THE

Sumac

READER

THE
Sumac
READER

Introductions by
Dan Gerber & Jim Harrison

. . .

Edited by Joseph Bednarik

Michigan State University Press
East Lansing

Copyrights for all work included in *The Sumac Reader* are held by the individual authors, publishers, and estates. Michigan State University Press and the editor gratefully acknowledge the generosity of those poets, writers, publishers, and estates who granted permission to reprint copyrighted material in this anthology. Thanks are also due to Dr. Peter Berg of Special Collections at the Michigan State University Library who graciously provided access to Dan Gerber's archived papers.

The cover image, "Moonrise III," is an oil on boards (1981) courtesy of Russell Chatham. The *Sumac* owl logo is by Ray Jansma. Book and cover design by M. Rae Thompson.

All Michigan State University Press books are produced on paper which meets the requirements of American National Standard of Information Sciences—permanence of paper for printed materials ANSI Z39.48–1984.

Michigan State University Press
East Lansing, MI 48823-5202

02 01 00 99 98 97 96 1 2 3 4 5 6 7 8 9

ISBN: 0-87013-462-0 / paperback
ISBN: 0-87013-427-2 / cloth

Library of Congress Cataloging-in-Publication Data

Bednarik, Joseph.
    The Sumac reader / introductions by Dan Gerber & Jim Harrison / edited by Joseph Bednarik
        p. cm.
    ISBN 0-87013-427-2 (cloth)— ISBN 0-87013-462-0 (pbk.)
    1. American literature—20th century
    2. American poetry—20th century

PS536.2 .S86 1996
810.8/0054 20   96018730
                                             CIP

ACKNOWLEDGMENTS

Permission to reprint material in *The Sumac Reader* has been generously granted by the contributing authors as well as the following:

"The Busride" by Paul Blackburn, from *The Collected Poems of Paul Blackburn*, edited by Edith Jarolim. Copyright © 1985 by Joan Blackburn. Reprinted by permission of Persea Books, Inc.

"You can't grip years, Postume...," a translation of Horace by Basil Bunting, from *The Complete Poems*, edited by Richard Caddel. Copyright © 1994 The Estate of Basil Bunting. Reprinted by permission of Oxford University Press.

"Re-Acquaintance" and "The Ravine" by Hayden Carruth, from *Collected Shorter Poems, 1946–1991*. Copyright © 1992 by Hayden Carruth. Reprinted by permission of Copper Canyon Press.

"White and the River" by Siv Cedering, from *Letters from the Floating World*. Copyright © 1984 by Siv Cedering. Reprinted by permission of the University of Pittsburgh Press.

"Gulls" and "In the Full Light of Day" by Eugene Guillevic, from *Selected Poems*. Copyright © 1969 by Denise Levertov Goodman and Eugene Guillevic. Reprinted by permission of New Directions Publishing Corp.

"Morning in Padova" and "Paestum" by Richard Hugo, from *Making Certain it Goes On: The Collected Poems of Richard Hugo*. Copyright © 1984 by Richard Hugo. Reprinted by permission of W.W. Norton & Company, Inc.

"I Was Sitting," a translation of Juan Ramón Jiménez by Robert Bly, from *Lorca and Jiménez: Selected Poems*, chosen and translated by Robert Bly, Beacon Press, Boston. Copyright © 1973 by Robert Bly. Reprinted with his permission.

"The Dead Shall Be Raised Incorruptible" by Galway Kinnell, from *The Book of Nightmares*. Copyright © 1971 by Galway Kinnell. Reprinted by permission of Houghton Mifflin Co. All rights reserved.

"Wanting the Moon I" and "Wanting the Moon II" by Denise Levertov, from *Poems 1968–1972*. Copyright © 1970 by Denise Levertov. Reprinted by permission of New Directions Publishing Corp.

"Notes for a Later Canto" and "Notes for Canto CXI" by Ezra Pound, from *The Cantos of Ezra Pound*. Copyright © 1934, 1971 by Ezra Pound. Reprinted by permission of New Directions Publishing Corp.

"The Blue Ghazals: 9/21/68 and 9/23/68:i" by Adrienne Rich, from *Collected Early Poems: 1950–1970*. Copyright © 1993 by Adrienne Rich. Reprinted by permission of the author and W.W. Norton & Company, Inc.

"The Beards" by Jerome Rothenberg, from *Poland/1931*. Copyright © 1974 by Jerome Rothenberg. Reprinted by permission of New Directions Publishing Corp.

"Wait for Me" by James Tate, from *Selected Poems*. Copyright © 1991 by Wesleyan University Press. Reprinted by permission of University Press of New England.

"Love Letter Postmarked Van Beethoven" by Diane Wakoski, from *Emerald Ice: Selected Poems 1962–1987*. Copyright © 1988 by Diane Wakoski. Reprinted by permission of Black Sparrow Press.

"Today I Will Admire" copyright © by Paul Zweig. Reprinted by permission of Georges Borchardt, Inc. for The Estate of Paul Zweig.

PREFACE

OLD LITERARY MAGAZINES are a cultural treasure. They also tend to be stacked along the lowest shelves at used-book stores. Since many of these magazines are saddle-stitched, a mildly interested party cannot just lean back and scan the spines for titles. It takes commitment to kneel down and dig.

I was an undergraduate and kneeling in a Philadelphia bookshop when a fellow customer took interest in my selections. He introduced himself as a dealer and claimed to have an extensive collection of "little magazines" for sale through his catalog. We shared a pleasant conversation, which eventually worked into a proposition: He needed work done around his house and offered me $10.00 an hour to help, payable in literature. That Saturday I turned garden beds in exchange for early issues of *kayak*, *Stony Brook*, *Hanging Loose*, *Lillabulero*, *Alcheringa*, *The Reaper*, and *Spit in the Ocean*. I reached for a copy that read *Sumac* down the spine. "Sorry," the dealer said, "I can't break up the run." There were nine volumes priced at $100. I leafed through several copies and became impressed with the production quality, the writers who were represented, and the poems. I left twenty dollars on account and planned to work the next Saturday for the complete run.

During the week's reading a letter surfaced in a *kayak* correspondence column from Jim Harrison: "In the past two years since I've been co-editing *Sumac* I've been amazed at the number of people who want evidently a 'career' in poetry.... It is obvious that too many people are reading biographies of Dylan Thomas and Roethke when Beddoes and Rimbaud would provide a more accurate synopsis of a career." *This is going to be good,* I thought, and called the dealer to confirm our schedule. "By the way," he said, "I sold that set."

"Of *Sumac*? I thought we had an agreement?"

"A collector from New York wanted it. You don't say no to collectors from The City."

I gave instant notice, retreated to the public library, and found Sumac Press listed in a publishers reference book. I sent a letter to Fremont, Michigan, and in return received an order form: Copies of the magazine could still be purchased for $2.00 each and *yes*, every issue was available. I bought a set, savored each discovery, then bought another set and shipped it to a friend. I included copies of the order form in all my correspondence. I wanted *Sumac* to find homes, new readers, to become dog-eared, underlined, and filled with margin notes; in short, I wanted all the remaining copies to be bought up and distributed before my dealer heard word of this mother lode out in Michigan.

. . .

Independent literary magazines—those outside the support of a university—are founded with passion and enjoy a short (hopefully brilliant) existence. The average life-span seems to be seven issues. The inaugural issue is constructed easefully; the second issue arises from momentum; any third issue brings with it the thankless and oftentimes costly work of publishing.

The work of *Sumac* involved the founding co-editors Dan Gerber and Jim Harrison, Tom McGuane as the fiction editor (final six issues), the East Coast/New York editors James Randall (first four issues) and Robert Vas Dias (last four issues), Ray Hoagland as Art Director (seven issues) and James Austin as Managing Editor (five issues). For their combined efforts from fall 1968 to fall 1971 these men produced nine volumes and presented nearly 900 poems, translations, experimental fictions, book reviews and criticism from over 250 contributors. *Library Journal* recognized *Sumac* as "one of the best little magazines now being published.... The whole is professionally edited, and a fine balance is struck between the younger avant-garde poets and the older members of the faculty."

Sumac's efforts toward, and achievement of, that "fine balance" were not always graciously recognized. In the third issue an "Editorial Note" from Gerber and Harrison read, in part:

> Some criticism has been directed at us for being what we are not, and we shall remain so. We are not *Caterpillar, Io, kayak, The Sixties, Tri-Quarterly*, or *Poetry*. They are. If we evolve any distinct personality it will be as a magazine where poets need not worry if their work is "right for us." There are enough magazines, perhaps, with very singular interests and directions, almost mouthpieces for particular schools and groups. And some of those old outworn enormities like *Partisan, Kenyon* and *Hudson* are still around, but no magazine that publishes all sides of the geographical rifts in American poetry. This might not be possible without alienating all parties, we'll certainly find out. It may be heretical to say so but poems are more interesting than poets, collections of poets, manifestoes, main currents, and eddies. We hope to offer an energetic catholicity.

What *The Sumac Reader* hopes to offer, twenty-five years after the final issue, is both the energy and catholicity that Dan Gerber and Jim Harrison envisioned for their magazine. If this book does its job, readers will be inspired to kneel and search floor-level shelves at used-book stores. Those who are fortunate enough to find copies of *Sumac* will no doubt discover work they feel should have been included in this book. Rather than apologize for any editorial blind spots, I invite readers to include those writings: Paste the poems on the inside covers or write them out on pages with generous white space. It would be an honor if *The Sumac Reader* lived up to *Sumac*'s subtitle: "An Active Anthology."

—Joseph Bednarik

CONTENTS

INTRODUCTIONS

DAN GERBER

IN 1967 JIM HARRISON AND I conceived the idea of a magazine that might transcend the factions and exclusivities that seemed to us inimical to our vision of what American poetry should be, following the tyranny of The New Criticism. Whitman set the example. What we wanted to present in *Sumac* was a largeness of spirit, a poetry with no "elegance or affect or originality to hang in the way like curtains between us and the rest...a poetry to shame the silliness out of us." Of course we still had a good deal of silliness and would gather more along the way, as did Whitman himself, but we hoped to find a body of work in America in the late Sixties that would make that silliness seem minor in context.

This had been done rather well by Robert Bly and James Wright in *The Fifties* and *The Sixties*, but still there was a kind of "them and us" attitude between East Coast and West Coast, Olsonites and Academics, Deep Imagists and Objectivists, that seemed to us beside the point.

Jim and I had known each other only slightly at Michigan State in the late Fifties. Several years after I graduated and Jim had been awarded his M.A., Clyde Henson, a professor whose bearing and command of American literature had inspired us both, handed me a copy of *Plain Song*, Jim's first collection of poems, and I discovered a voice beginning to master the kind of power and clarity I hoped for my own work. I wrote to Jim in Long Island, where he had taken a job as assistant to Herbert Weisenger, another professor and mentor from our days at Michigan State who had become head of the English Department of the State University of New York at Stony Brook. Our friendship grew through a two-year correspondence and we finally met face to face when my doorbell rang early on New Year's Eve 1967. Jim had been awarded a National Endowment grant and he and his wife, Linda, stopped by during their hunt for a house in northern Michigan in which to spend the following year.

After that first meeting, we continued to discuss our ideas for the magazine through letters and phone calls, and it was at Jim and Linda's kitchen table in Stony Brook, during a visit to them the following spring, that I suggested the name, *Sumac*. It was a tree long familiar to us both, not a particularly glamorous tree, but tough and ubiquitous. (It wasn't Camus spelled backwards, as has often been suggested.) We liked the sound of "sumac," the way it looked on the page, and we knew without hesitation that it was the name for our magazine.

Of course we were naive. We couldn't have attempted such an eclecticism if we hadn't been. We were full of Whitman, Lorca, Rimbaud, Neruda, Apollinaire and Yeats, guided by our own "blind stupefied hearts." We were enthralled by the idea of seeing our own work in the context of what we hoped would be the best work of our time, of seeing it handsomely in print and available to any who felt, as we did, the need for it.

Fortunately our enthusiasm, and the respect Jim was already gaining as a poet, won the sympathy of our mentors, among the most important voices of our time, who honored us with their new work. Their generosity provided a platform for many emerging young writers, so the pages of *Sumac* enjoyed a wide-ranging association. As Robert Duncan once told us in amazement, and probably also with some amusement, writers in *Sumac* frequently found themselves in a company they would never have imagined.

We were guided by what we thought was good and courageous and necessary. Word spread fairly quickly. We received writing, unsolicited, from poets both prominent and obscure, including, through the good graces of James Laughlin, even Ezra Pound. Within the first year, the mail was often bringing upwards of 150 manuscripts a week. As the junior partner, I would sort through the mountains of paper and separate out what seemed to me the good from the not-so-good. Though it was laborious, those distinctions were fairly easy. Choosing the best from all that was worthy was far more difficult. I would mail a dozen or so manuscripts each week to Jim, and once or twice a month I would make the two-and-a-half hour drive north to his rented farmhouse near Lake Leelanau, or he would drive down to Fremont where we would read and walk and talk over what we thought might be the most vital work we had with which to build each new issue.

We were becoming conscious of our world through language, in love with its possibilities and the kind of lightning it could sometimes strike. I'm sure there are a few things we regret publishing and probably a great many more we regret passing over. Looking back all those years now, I'm proud of what we did publish and pleased that *Sumac* has been rediscovered.

JIM HARRISON

"*Sumac*, THY NAME IS LIKE A BELL." Or not. I still have uncomfortable night thoughts of the U.S. Mail dropping off manuscripts in a dump truck. All too soon, say within a year of our slow start, *Sumac* became a rough trade operation, requiring an amount of time and energy I was ill-prepared to offer. It was years later before I clearly understood that editing in itself is a gift, a very rare talent indeed. But at the time, the overwhelming impulse was to create a magazine that I'd actually like to read, and I had not yet admitted that all the brains and craft for doing so resided in my partner, Dan Gerber.

I'm clumsy with dates so will make no mention of them. My life is divided into dogs and ours at the time of *Sumac* was an English Pointer named Missy. I dedicated my first novel to her, along with Tom McGuane who, as a dog man, was quite comfortable with her company. She died at age five, about as long as the magazine lasted and, inevitably, I think of the two together: fellow creatures, unruly, occasionally graceful, but all too mortal.

It is interesting to recall the magazines I cherished as a late teen which specifically formed my first ambitions for *Sumac*. It's also embarrassing when you consider the dimensions, the utter unreality of the dream. I most loved *Botteghe Oscure*, edited by Marguerite Caetani out of Rome. Only about one third of each issue was in English which made it attractively mysterious as I had no foreign languages. Another magazine I admired was the *New Directions* annual, and to a slightly lesser extent, Robert Bly's *The Fifties*, and its successor, *The Sixties*. I was distinctly a northern midwesterner and the latter magazine helped me understand that even with a rural background I had a shot at being a poet. But back to editing. I worshipped eclecticism and if you have severely limited editorial talents you better limit your focus, which we refused to do. Much in the manner in which I view movies, I sort of liked and disliked manuscripts at the same time. There's something appealing in the idea that anyone has bothered to learn (rarely well) how to write poetry or fiction in the first place. I did not properly apprehend at the time that the M.F.A. craze was growing like a Ponzi Scheme and that publication in our magazine was actually thought to be a credential. Added to this is the novel idea that there have always been vastly more poets than there have been readers of poetry.

The first two years of the magazine were relatively graceful despite my well-founded fears that I was a maladept editor. The first year I was on a National Endowment grant (back when they were enough to support that length of time), and when that was exhausted, I was awarded a Guggenheim, my family's last piece of security before the harrowing ten years that followed during which we averaged less than ten grand a year. Only recently it's been a bit comic to reflect that the much beleaguered National Endowment gave me my start and in the last fifteen years or so through the medium of screenplays I've paid enough income tax to support a couple hundred such grants. I'm sure this is true of others.

When the gravy train collided with reality I was much less helpful to Dan, what with having to make a living. Nonetheless, we tried hard whether at his farm or my own, sifting through the huge piles of manuscripts, an intellectualized version of gold panning. I certainly have no regrets over the enormous time spent. We were at the age when energy was in good supply and I trust the assemblage in this anthology justifies the effort. I only gradually understood that the temperament that made me an unsuccessful teacher, also limited my usefulness as an editor. I was simply unable to fully concentrate at the time on any activity or work other than the work I was creating.

I still own the firmest belief in the idea of the small press. With the exception of my first three books of poetry and my *Selected & New Poems* I have always chosen a small press for my ensuing volumes of poetry, and this when I was welcome anywhere. New York is having trouble enough maintaining a viable interest in the literary novel. Poetry gets lost there, or is published as if it were the gospel according to *The New Yorker*. Time has proven the vitality lies elsewhere where it can properly germinate. Later on it doesn't really matter if Knopf prints the collected poems for fifty bucks because the audience has been gradually accumulating or accreted, and not very far down the line it doesn't matter who the publisher is, just that the good work saw the light of day.

CHARLES SIMIC

How to Psalmodise

1. The Poet.

Someone awake when others are sleeping,
Asleep when others are awake.
An illiterate who signs everything with an X.
A man about to be hanged cracking a joke.

2. The Poem.

It is a piece of meat
Carried by a burglar
To distract a watchdog.

Second Avenue Winter

When the horses were no longer found in dreams,
And the village virgins ceased riding them naked,
When their mane ceased to resemble sea-foam,
And the twitching of their ears no longer prophesied
   great battles,

Just then a horse came pulling a wagon
Piled up high with old mattresses,
Bent under a halo of yellow steam
On thick sturdy legs the color of winter twilight,
Partly a ghost, partly a poor man's burial,
Bearing with each step the heaviness
Of a dumb and unknown animal anguish.

The fresh snow sobbed under the hoofs of the last horse,
The wagon-wheels whined their ancient lineage
Of country roads, of drunks left lying in the mud,
Of million years of poverty and cold wind.

I, too, went after them
With a slow shuffle
Of sweet psalmodic thoughts,
Like a drunk Bible salesman,

Thinking of the old negro driver,
Of the insanity that makes him keep
A horse in the city,
Of their night and their supper,
Its ritual and secret life
Where I wish to be anointed.

The Wedding

Mother gives me
to the daylight on the threshold.

I have the steam of my breath
for a carnation.

Poverty my bride,
you have the lightest step.

Ax

Whoever swings an ax
Knows the body of man
Will again be covered with fur.
The stench of blood and swamp water
Will return to its old resting places.
They'll spend their winters
Sleeping like the bears.
The skin on the throats of their women
Will grow coarse. He who cannot
Grow teeth, will not survive.
He who cannot howl
Will not find his pack...

These dark prophecies were gathered,
Unknown to myself, by my body
Which understands historical probabilities,
Being itself, in its essence, without a future.

JIM HEYNEN

Coyote

WHAT MAKES THE OLD BOY TICK?
Nothing that anybody knows how to talk about.
Sixty feet away, between two large stacks of scrap wood, the
old boy is picking around for the larger pieces. His lunch break.
Half a sandwich protrudes from his face as one hand works
through the lumber. The dark red veins on his face are close
to the surface. Sweat welts shine on his forehead. The two men
in blue workshirts watch him from their perch on top a three-
foot stack of finished plywood. Curiously, as workmen in a zoo
studying the movements of an animal they have known for years
but whose actions are still fascinating.

He'll take the larger pieces out to his truck. They say he carves
things out of them, but nobody knows for sure.

You mean—

Old boy knows wood though. Pick out a bird's-eye maple in
the woods quicker than anyone I know. Used to be one of the
best loggers in the Upper Peninsula until he lost his hand under
a chain, loading white pine. Has been working in the mill here
ever since. Cleaning up. Learned how to use a broom, but never
an ax again. His name really is Logman, you know. Victor. Get
to know him. You'll learn something.

Summers?

Yeah. Come November and he'll up and quit. Go to his cabin
on Bear Creek and you'll hardly see him again until spring.
Think he'd do just the opposite—work in the winter. But Vic
just holes up for the winter. Sort of a winter camper. Makes you
wonder about cabin fever. They say he does some work with
junk-iron, but I never seen any of it. Nobody hardly sees him.
Matt's afraid he's just going to up and die there one of these
years. But every spring, depending on how soon the snow's gone,
he'll show up here and Matt will hire him on.

Victor takes the larger pieces out to his truck, a huge stack of one-inch scraps stacked up to the size of a bushel basket on the handless arm. The arm is strong and stands at a right angle to his body. Into the air like a great elm topped by lightning. He wears a patch of leather taped over the tip to save it from bruises. The springs of the old truck grunt as he steps onto the rear hitch to get to the truck-box floor where he stacks the scraps. He looks up and to the west, sniffs the air, throws up a handful of dust, watches it on the wind, looks to the west again, reaches down and unfolds a canvas tarp over his lumber. At 1:00 the saws start and no one tries to speak over the whine of steel on wood. Victor moves easily about his work, stroking the floor firmly with the broom in his good hand.

One afternoon in November, Victor sees sundogs cradle the afternoon sun like colorful blankets. Thirteen sandhill cranes circle over the forest until from the north the fourteenth comes and they fly together south, leaving only their strange haunting cry on the wind. Final pay, and he moves slowly through the tall grass of the clearing near his cabin, his old truck—black and rusted—parked at the edge of the drive. He cradles his rifle and thinks of his wife, long dead.

Around the cabin are old pieces of scrap-iron, pieces of old cars and machinery, a makeshift block-and-tackle hoist for lifting iron to and from his truck. The cabin is small, made of large logs which have turned a uniform gray. Its lines are straight, sturdy. It has one large window overlooking Bear Creek, just one hundred yards down the northern slope from his cabin. One door. Inside are two workbenches, one for iron and one for wood. A stone fireplace, a Monarch woodstove, a wooden bunkbed, hand-made cabinets. Buckets. Clothing hung on nails. Two gas lanterns hanging from the log beams.

Down into the woods for winter firewood. Four-inch logs broken by wind or age. He drags them home under his handless arm to save strength in the other for sawing. Noticing much in the process. Deer sign. Partridge nests. Always looking closely under fallen logs. Beneath one is a black beetle.

It is fall, black beetle.

The insect does not move, cradled in the small cavity it has burrowed in the soil, its dark wings gleaming with moisture.

Good place, my idea of it.

The log slips from his good hand and falls with a thud on the beetle.

Unch.

He pulls at the log with both arm and hand. The beetle is whole, untouched. He drops the log, knowing.

Winter comes on. In the town of Manitac, Michigan, determination in the way men walk. Snow tires, chains, on cars. Heavy jackets, thick gloves, high boots. Men look at each other's clothing to see who knows best. Old women stare out from kitchen windows measuring the snow against their memories. Old men in old houses, their wives dead, make love to calloused hands. In the woods, deer approach the sound of the chain saw, too hungry and weak not to trust. In the woods. In the woods. Victor. On snowshoes, his rifle cradled on the arm with no hand, the stub well covered with leather and wool.

The coldest part is the part that ain't there.

Slow, easy walk, swinging the snowshoes wide with each step. Short, stocky body, deliberate and slow as one who has not gone far and is not going much farther. On his back a plastic-covered deer license of four years ago.

I don't hunt, see. The deer come to me.

Black stocking cap. Red wool jacket. Large head deep in his shoulders, the shoulders rising sharply upward like padding, like birds' wings. The face rough, not with bones but flesh. Down near the creek, Bear Creek, he stops and waits. The deer come to him. A large buck moves past, its broad white tail against its gray thighs. He shoots from behind. The forehead explodes and it falls, muscles tight and quivering. Bone and tissue from its forehead. Blood from its mouth. He carries the meat in quarters to his cabin, his good hand dark with the blood. Meat enough for eight weeks. He will not shoot until then.

But you see it's not like it used to be in the woods when nobody gonna be there except they have good reason. Now with car and roadplow and snowmobile and what-have-you, sonsabitches get maybe quarter mile from my cabin and come walking out here because they think they can hunt my forty. Once I'm fishing down by the crick and on the comeback, I meet couple of them from town—town kids—and tell them what-for they don't like it. So one night after dark I hear, Hey Vic, come out here a minute. Well, I think it kids but I don't go out there where it's ice-storming that night and they might easy jump me. But next day I see the tracks and they was grown-man size. They probably wouldn't killed me, but they would worked me over. No reason at the time why I didn't go out there. I guess I wasn't supposed to I guess. Some bad people up here nowadays, my idea of it. Keep my thirty-ought-six loaded now. Next time I'll go out. If they keep coming, I'll raise up on them a little bit. Matt say, Careful I don't shoot nobody up there. I told him not to worry. I ain't gonna shoot no human being. Not unless they crowd me too much.

Finally in a bad winter a man can go down to his shoulders in the snow. Only his crotch to hold him up if he doesn't have snowshoes. From the snow-plowed highway the snow appears harmlessly smooth and shallow as it spreads back into the woods. But the road is like a shore line. The snow deepens like a lake as a man moves into it. In the woods the deer can move into trouble simply by walking on wrong places. They often gather near or on railways to escape the deep snow only to find a different and more violent death.

Four foot of snow in the woods. Dug out this morning. Funny how grass and some weeds are still green under there. Matt wouldn't believe this, but I found a whippoorwill out there this morning. Not dead neither. Just barely moving. Like it had been sleeping. Don't know why it didn't make it south. But it make it this far through the winter, so I let it there. Wouldn't be there if it wasn't supposed to be I figured it. Sky is good now though. Won't be no more snow for at least two days. Some deer starving. Game wardens cutting some tree on state land for feed. That's better than dropping hay. Deer not used to that kind of feed in the winter. Better to cut tree. Too much cutting of small tree in summer what I say....

The Bradleys are a family of three. Their cabin is the nearest to Victor's. They have not met him, but know the cabin near Bear Creek belongs to an old logger named Victor Logman. The father likes the name. He imagines the title Logger Logman, which is almost as good as his uncle's name, Greggor McGreggor, who lived for years in what is now his and his family's summer cabin. They have remodeled the cabin, putting in more windows and wiring it for electricity, but they have a picture of Greggor hanging on the wall, showing him standing in front of his cabin as it appeared twenty-five years ago. They have also kept on one wall a framed four-leaf clover which Greggor cut out of a magazine twenty years ago.

Greggor and me used to log what's now Kingston Plains. Good timber then. White pine five feet across. Rough place up there around Germfast. Used to be bad fights in camp. Half-breed Indian Frenchmen—we called them bow-and-arrow Frenchmens—used to come down on the Swedes and Scotch for talking what they thought was broken. What was mostly is that you can't find no pussy so you find a fight. Greggor got stabbed once. Waited six months until he was healthy enough to get back at the man with his bare hands. Broke the guy's jaw and some ribs. Bare hands. Regular fella, Greggor. Regular fella. Had his first heart attack the year I lost it. We both bought our forties then. Dollar an acre. Almost lost them for the taxes. All the wood for the cabins is off the land. You know, seemed what Greggor could smell a coyote for over half a mile. Usually at night, sitting outside, he'd say, I smell coyote piss. And like as not, there'd be coyote howling in a minute. Not many coyote and foxes anymore. They're starting to go right into town to find feed. Most of them killed on the roads. Never forget. Greggor always listened to the news. Always knew the news. Big fella. He'd be alive today if they hadn't put him in Old

People Home. Not natural for Greggor. His kin got his place now. Couple and a boy. They're Sugar Beets, I think. Detroit. Never met them. They come weekends in the summer when I'm at the mill....

The sound of the Bradley's car and trailer carries over the snow as sound over water. Squeak of tires on hard-frozen snow. The smooth Buick engine. Then the shovelling in.

You listen careful at night and you can hear the deer walk. Deer is noisier than you think. You can hear the half-moons of their hind hoof click together when they step down. Greggor could hear it too. Least he says he could. I think I had the ears and he had the nose. Matt would just laugh. Said it didn't make no difference anyways. Matt was best with fish. And he had good eyes. Says there's gold spots on the wings of sandhill cranes. Almost like the spots on a fawn, he says. But we never got close enough to know for sure. Nobody of us ever got no bear. Never tried too hard neither. Ain't one of us really wanted to bother them. And you only see bear in the summer. We was always busy then. Once just before I come up for the winter there was Sugar Beets had shot this bear and took him to town and hung him up on big saw horses right in front of Herb's 50 Bar and was inside getting drunk. Had the mouth all taped shut to keep out the flies. Kids all around seeing what they'd done. That bear had the bullet hole right in the center of his forehead. Right between the eyes. Only one way you can get a bear right between the eyes. At night with spot light. Only way you'll catch them looking at you like that. Sonsabitches. Skinned bear looks just like human beings. Folks, mostly Sugar Beets, will set by the dump for hours watching for the bear to come....

At the Bradley's cabin the windows begin to frost as the temperature inside rises from the heat of the oil-burner. The mother is busy unpacking food, her long blond hair falling on her blue sweater. The son has books on the table, one on taxidermy; new boots; new gloves. His eyes are intense, alert. He is a good student. The father is pouring fuel into the Jungers heater, his pipe in his teeth unlit, a smile spreading from the pipe to the corners of his mouth. They are soon dressing to go back out, the son and the father, going out to the trailer, unloading their snowmobile, black and sleek in the starlight. The machine rests quietly on the snow, looking like an oversized soapbox racer with runners under it. Then the engine whines like the sound of a chain saw, the father takes the steering bars, and the large cleated rubber drive band spins in the snow. They are gone into the dark woods as a new boat upon water, into the deeper snow. In the opposite direction from Victor.

Seems that everybody nowadays have their hobby. Well, I was a kid I made whistles from willow sticks. Snowmobile is an expensive toy. Matt heard there's over hundred thousand of them in Michigan now. Boy of Steve McPharland stuck his leg out on one and almost lost his nuts. Ripped him up the middle. And there ain't as many deer around here no more neither. They run them over or catch them and shoot them. Used to be a lot more deer around here. Bc in the woods cutting and you'd see them peeping around the tree waiting for you to leave so they could eat off the leaves....

And then they are at the edge of a great clearing, a seventy-five yard wide swath through the woods that stretches from horizon to horizon. It is the clearing made for the huge gas pipeline laid in three years ago. Into the center of the wide snow path and they level off the machine into the infinite stretch. From the opposite direction more lights. Five lights moving in formation towards them. The outside lights lead. The center light is the farthest back. Lights in the V-formation of geese—moving backwards. The son and father stop, turn off their light, and watch. In the center of the V, a coyote zig-zagging for freedom.

They're harmful to wildlife.

Who?

Coyotes.

I could stuff him and mount him on wood.

In the center of the backward V-flight of machines the coyote moves as a swimmer in water. Slow, ludicrous maneuvers, its gray coat dark on the snow. Following its summer habit of dodging scrub oak and trees. Moving by memory, its nose down for places to hide, striking the snow as the blade of a snowplow.

In a moment there are six in formation, the son and father waved in by the friendly machine men. Six lights in the moving formation. With a sudden surge of speed, the son and father move out, break the formation to kill. At fifty miles per hour the machine strikes the coyote. Thud of hitting a log. Twisted and broken upon impact, the coyote goes down in the snow. The machines stand idling around it. Its intestines are wrapped around its neck. Blood soaks up to the surface of snow.

Jesus Christ! What a smell! What the hell do they eat? Smells like it's been dead for six weeks. Jesus Christ! Can anything be that sour? Don't touch it, Son. It's probably poisoned or something. Probably was dying already. Jesus Christ, what a stench!

Back in the cabin the night grows quiet around them. The son pages through his books to see how it might have been mounted. How far does the neck tilt back when it yelps? How far does its mouth open? The three retire with the silence of stars on the snow. The son waits for the snores of his parents, waits for a chance to masturbate. Instead, later—much later— he hears a shuffling of blankets, his parents' quick motions of love. Then the whispering voice of his mother. Wait. Wait. And silence. The son lies tense in his knowledge of silence.

The morning sun. It has not snowed for three days. From the snow the glitter of shattered glass. The son wipes off one of the several windows. Outside, the tamarack tree, its needles gone for the winter. Son and mother watch the gray nuthatch on its trunk, dancing its upside-down dance.

Do you know why it clings upside-down from the tree?

No. No. I do not.

Its enemy comes up from the bottom. It must watch the base of the tree.

Is that really why?

Yes, Son, why else?

At noon, snow starts to fall, and the Bradleys prepare for a ride. Bright colors red yellow blue as they ride their machine through the woods. They are taking a round-about route, their scenic route as they call it. Zig-zagging through the woods past spruce, cedar, pine, balsam, and birch. They approach the blacktop road. The snow is coming down faster. Alert to a sound not their own, they wait at the side of the road. An old truck slowly approaches. The handless arm is steering, the other holds a trip-rope. As the truck is idling past them, the wife lifts a red glove to wave. Suddenly, the trip-rope jerks, and a huge wooden arm is in motion. Two hundred miles per hour, it swings from the truck-box floor. All three are dead upon impact, their machine shattering with them. Flames burst up and the cold flesh burns in the snow.

Back at his cabin Victor undoes his contraption. An eighteen-foot plank with a swivel on one end mounted to the truck-box floor, free to swing out fourteen feet from the side of the truck. To the swinging end is mounted a heavy car-bumper. Twelve garage-door springs mounted to the back of the cab on one end, to the center of the plank on the other. The plank was drawn back to the full tightness of all twelve springs. The trip-rope released it. It had never been tested. Without an object to strike, the plank would have continued around and smashed the truck cab.

Using his hoist, Victor drops all parts into the fresh snow. Each sinks down as in water. The snow is falling still harder. The worst storm of the season. The old truck sits in its place, snow rising up around it.

Days pass. In the town of Manitac, men talk of slippery roads and hit-and-run drivers. Men driving '66 Chevys explain their dented bumpers.

In his cabin Victor works at his wood bench, then at his iron. The one window lets in little light. It is dark. He works slowly. The scraps of wood saved all summer. Nailed to walls. Reinforced with iron. Each year the walls grow stronger and thicker with new wood and iron. Each year the snow may be deeper. The cabin stronger. The walls thicker and thicker. Each year the cabin slightly smaller and safer. The process of knowing and making a place. It is what one must know in winter. In the woods.

Spring comes. Always late in the Upper Peninsula. April and the young frogs' song is inhumanly high and sustained. With May the frogs' song lowers, their voices fall to the level of men's. Victor moves out. It is the time of motion and light. When he must move with the tide of the earth, with a strength not his own. He moves slowly out. Closes his cabin. In the wet earth outside is a hole, the size of a small rat's. A few inches from it, a shell, blue as the sky or a lake. The shell of the land crab.

Have you come up or gone under?
He picks up the shell, brittle, blue in his hand. He moves toward his truck, and the sawmill.

REBECCA NEWTH

Origins Own You

           I must get a family murder
    out of my mind.
must purify make clear. must start a novel
    feel the weight of the phrase
        as it leaves
    feel the ear's weight
        the weight of the heart
    have you ever written without the mind?

    had carnal knowledge of your own
        delightful sentences
    the delight of the ears
        the weight of the heart's felt expressions
    the weight, even, of the right arm
        behind the pencil
    giving acclaim or affirmation
the eyes' physical beauty that day
    or weary, perhaps, you shrugged off depression

life made so many impressions on me
    I was like a wave
everyone crosses, or, like lava
    not cooling.

"Hannibal over the mountains..."

Hannibal over the mountains,
between the great blades of mountains leaning back on steeper
ascents of Hannibal's framed by sky —
how he would smash these to build a road.
Looking back, he sees enough to pity —
whole communities of moss, flowers fanned up in the crevices,
his own soul barely escapes a hammer still trailing a glove.
Yet, going forward, his mind fetches out among cities
where he manages to occupy beds, boats, markets, wheels,
smoke, hats, the faces of policemen reddened by cold.
And looking out one night on a scattering of men in dreary helmets
he is overwhelmed by their sky.
How clearly I see your costumes, my husband, to whom poems
keep occurring.

PAUL BLACKBURN

The Busride

The 26 kilometers
between the city and this village
used to take an hour-and-a-half.

The new driver
a young man
from Estallenchs
makes the same trip in an hour.
The old man's been
relegated down to ticket-taker.

1 hour
Neither rain nor fog nor low-lying cloud on those
      mountains etc.

1 hour

But the new man crosses himself
like any woman before starting,
a big cross,
wide   slow   and sure.
And despite the breakneck weight
of his big foot on the accelerator
his passengers ride
                    confident and relaxed.

HAYDEN CARRUTH

Re-Acquaintance

Kevin, Kevin Rooney, is it you?
come back like this in a title—

    "For K. R. Who Killed Himself
    in Charles Street Jail"

a poem by Gregory Corso/

        you, Kevin?
That day 15 years ago, front page *Mirror*
the unforgivable pix, you hanging there
face down in the barred iron corner
like a sad flag, you 'child of dark'
Corso calls you, and I say it too, Child of Dark—
I wanted to write something then for Chicago's sake,
nights of your most handsome Irish head asking
for poems nobody could write, nobody, such sorrows.
You held the automatic to your temple and pulled the
WHAM!—nothing happened, the damn thing wouldn't fire
so you waited two years, moved to the Village, and
did it in Charles Street with your belt.
        I stood
reading the *Mirror*; not reading, looking; ward six.
You had written once to the asylum, a forlorn letter.
Now what could I write from there, that wordless place?
I had a lousier day than usual, and a week later
electroshock wiped you out—until now—
now, Kevin, my Child of Dark. Drooped Flag.

The Ravine

Stones, brown tufted grass, but no water,
it is dry to the bottom. A seedy eye
of orange hawkweed blinks in sunlight
stupidly, a mink bumbles away,
a ringnecked snake among stones lifts its head
like a spark, a dead young woodcock—
long dead, the mink will not touch it—
sprawls in the hatchment of its soft plumage
and clutches emptiness with drawn talons.
This is the ravine today. But in spring it
cascaded, in winter it filled with snow
until it lay hidden completely. In time,
geologic time, it will melt away
or deepen beyond recognition, a huge
gorge. These are what I remember and foresee.
These are what I see here every day,
not things but relationships of things,
quick changes and slow. These are my sorrow,
for unlike my bright admonitory friends
I see relationships, I do not see things.
These, such as they are, every day, every
unique day, the first in time and the last,
are my thoughts, the sequences of my mind.
I wonder what they mean. Every day,
day after day, I wonder what they mean.

Notes for Canto CXI

I, one thing, as relation to one thing;
    Hui sees relation to ten.
20 shillings to Wadsworth
    "in resentment." Town house in Hartford.
Roche-Guyon stoned to death at Gisors.
    Power to issue, au fond,
                to tax.
Directory cd. have made bulwark of Italy
post-bag B.
    Austerlitz
        Banque de France
           Mme de Genlis
Lannes did not enjoy sight of a battlefield.
Whole lesson of Talleyrand
                Wu
                Hsieh (heart's field)
                Szu
Enlarged his empire
    diminished his forces,
Ten years a blessing,
        five a nuisance,
that was Napoleon
with constitutional guarantees
           April 22nd.
"Very few interested"
    N. to Talleyrand, "in civilization."
So that Alexander asked Talleyrand what to do about France.
And "to change the meaning of words themselves from one
                conference to another."
                Oct. 31st, Wien

And 600 more dead at Quemoy—
        they call it political.

A nice quiet paradise,
        Orage held the basic was pity
            compassione,
                        Amor
Gold mermaid up from black water—
        Night against sea-cliffs
            the low reef of coral—
And the sand grey against undertow
        as Geryon—lured there—but in splendour,
Veritas, by anthesis, from the sea depth
        come burchiello in su la riva
The eyes holding trouble—
        no light
                ex profundis—
naught from feigning.
Soul melts into air,
                anima into aura,
                        Serenitas.

Coin'd gold
        also bumped off 8000 Byzantines
Edictum prologo
        Rothar.

Notes for a Later Canto

La faillite de François Bernouard, Paris
or a field of larks at Allègre,
    "es laissa cader"
so high toward the sun and then falling,
    "de joi sas alas"
to set here the roads of France.

Two mice and a moth my guides—
To have heard the farfalla gasping
    as toward a bridge over worlds.
That the kings meet in their island,
    where no food is after flight from the pole.
Milkweed the sustenance
    as to enter arcanum.

To be men not destroyers.

DAVID RAY

Li Po

Aye, he could hear what the heavens said,
But only when he was fat and stumbling with wine,
Only when he'd known what the true grief was,
And when he knew neither moon nor pool comforted,
When he knew nothing in nature would let him
Fly or flow away, and he was meant to stay
With his sorrow, on a hillside, looking back,
Poor wingless creature, poor round-faced dead man.

J.D. REED

The Chuck Berry Triptych

for Marlene

NOTES FROM THE CATALOGUE

Saw Maybellene in a Coupe de Ville

In the boiling
August of Kansas
I squat, sighting-in
the edge of U.S. 40,
her turtleback bumpy,
shimmering in alcohol.

At night the wheat crackles,
at noon the women buy bicycle
clips to fasten shotguns on pick-up
dashboards.

In a Lincoln I flash by radar
domes, giant golfballs, and grain
elevators shimmering in the exhaust
like twenty-mile Xanadus.

Past diners, past the lovers, past the sick,
wide-eyed druggists shot with cancer,
past cattle flopped on their sides
bloated with wet alfalfa;
straw floats in the small trickle
of a ravine.

As if I were a glacier, one
micro-millimeter thick and vertical
the country hums through my ice:

I fall sideways on the long grass,
a map-making machine; extruding
under pressure this landscape.

A linoleum knife slits
my vision temple to temple:
product, diaphragm,
the country uses me:
its sick whore-cow gone
romping in the sage,
its midnight son of song.

FIRST PANEL

> Cadillac settin' like a ton a lead,
> hundred and ten, half a mile ahead.

1.

The grandfathers hum in their tintypes,
stern faces of old-time shaving ads
in absolute confirmation of their chins:
can hands look that strong on weak men?

Two itinerants, toothpick suckers, advisors
to manual labor; the Keystone cops of all
our pioneers, firmly held for that breathless
instant in the photographer's head grip.

The wives posing beside them look as if
the dough were rising through the towel
or bacon burned in the pan. Hands to shoulders
of their men, they sniff in frothy blouses.

Blank the wombs that bred the parents,
half blank their seed; these four quarterbacks
balance on metal, browning like nails
and fade in their aging solutions.

      2.

One drunken granddaddy walked into the Kalamazoo
missed the bridge on applemash and mixed
his whiskey with brown water. A carp with belly
white as grandfather gulped air and fanned
in a fold of his shirt.

He leaked so much on the parlor carpet
they moved him to the porch, but still
the lid was sprung, and had to be refastened;
smell of bluegills in the new drapes,
and mincemeat pie at wakes.

The other drunk dug in his quarry
and drunk, dug on in the rain, his brandy
breath exploding with each pitch of the shovel;
a screendoor banged in the moisture, dislodged
the hill. He drowned in crushed stone.

Stiff in the pebbles, uncovered by his son,
the body was dragged home on a stone boat,
team snorting fog in the wet air, he was
dumped near the raccoon pelts, frozen in the rain
and stacked like plates.

3.

Death of rye sailors on seas of whiskey,
home to hearths of little profit,
grandfathers—their old blood on the plains
slick with nomads, blood roaring in trout streams,
in quick lime, blood of gold rush and steam power,
blood soon to be weakened on a gallows
of self-reliance:

Gravelman, motorman; old blood in livery stables,
over poker chips, pumping at consequence, drop
by godawful drop.

CENTER PANEL—Livonia, Michigan

Done got cloudy and started to rain,
tooted my horn for the passin' lane.
Rainwater blowin' up under my hood
knew that was doin' my motor good.

1.

Sunday evenings sparrows flash
shadows in the crumpled skylights of a factory.

No hum of winch
whine of electric starters
slap of belt or drill press gears:
no exhaust of hi-lo's ratchet of the Coke machine,
or rattle of wax paper, salt
on an egg.

Silent machines stand
in the slow haze, in films of oil,
old sawdust sopping grease
on the concrete:

machines that tomorrow will
rend flesh,
shear a finger, throw filings
in an eye.

2.

I've seen them drunk on the job,
Polacks sleeping on piles of dirty wipes.
Drunk enough to miss the time clock,
stumble in the parking lot
and faint delirious in their cars.

The day steward drank,
bought crackers from a machine
and sat with me talking shop
talk.

3.

grievance report:

My name is Dewey Thacker
of Pikesville, now of Livonia
with my wife and the kid
my first wife left.

I operate a wire straightener,
you know that,
which nips oil-tempered wire
to the tolerance you set.

In the morning I take
one fifteen minute break

and a half an hour for lunch
(you followed with a stopwatch once)

then the same in the afternoon
and sometimes I punch out too soon,

because the wire gets to my eyes
or the oil does. I can hardly see
to drive home sometimes, it hurts so.

I like the work, but the doctor
said that ointment wouldn't help:
can I change jobs?

I know I'll lose
seniority, but
that's life's
little
breaks.

4.

$4,000 and nothing down
with the G.I. Bill, there's
my Stingray see her glint.
Sure
the wife cries:
women.

THIRD PANEL
YELLOWSTONE WOMEN

O Maybellene, why can't you be true?
O Maybellene, why can't you be true?
You done started back doin' the things
you used to do.

1.

The glint of sun reflected from her glasses
cuts across my vision like the cut of Eskimo goggles.
Her tight mouth and tighter hair repress a mother

Nothing more dangerous than this female,
worse than the roaming bears at their trash cans;
her fat triceps hangs from the window of a camper,
veined, purple flesh: gunsight for her stare.

In the parking lot of the boiling mudpots
she disapproves competitors, the marriage bed,
the man who burps and all her kind
crunching toward the sights.

Her sen-sen breath, the daughter's snapshot,
a Venus flytrap who knows better than her doctor
finds the bubbling mud and sulphur obscene,
snorts to plague the every turn of my dance,
a bear.

2.

The wives of naval officers
whine their lives into cups of gin.

In kitchens, mired in electric
outlets, plugs and buttons,
they press palms to breasts
of gum, flanks of leather.

At tennis courts, at the beach
their only utterance is
"goodbye," wind blowing
white cotton dresses;

ships departing in the fog,
and in the kitchens
life as if

no men were in muddy water;
salt on the muzzles of ship's
cannon they cannot see...

3.

A cheerleader in Elko, Nevada,
works in the drive-in weekends,
no tomorrow on her glum,
slack lip.

It is the stare of something
to be used, the gaze of an instrument
in suede boots,

in Levis cut so tight
the crotch-welt pulls
into the seam of her delight
and lip meets lip of it again,
across the slim band of denim,

her bored eye rolls
over hot dogs and beer.

O Saturdays of sex at a mathclub dance,
sweatstink of the gymnasium and its
wrestling mats; she holds some buck tight
and watches the flag rot on the cold block wall.

Later the seniors dance in a basement
couple by couple disappearing.

Wine drunk now, her panties
flung across a sofa, as if
riderless they'd mounted,

she jolts to a bedroom
in a slant of buttocks
shedding planes of light.

4.

Muselet arched and stroking short,
come for me, for the country, slapping
rump to rump in your own time:

In the singular gravel of Nevada
the moon's robes unfold.

Have an eye for it woman!

The mad albino in your closet
knows, and waits with us, grinning:

your dreary sleep.

DAVID RAFAEL WANG

translations of Wang Wei, Li Po, and Shao Yeh

Poems of Separation

I. Wei City Song

In the city of Wei
    morning rain dampens the dust
By the traveler's lodge
    greener and greener the willows grow
Let me persuade you
    to drain just one more cup
Once out of the Yang fortress
    There will be no friends.

—Wang Wei (701–761)

II. Seeing Off at Bramble Gate

Traveling far to the Bramble Gate Mountain,
You came voyaging from the State of Ch'u.
The mountain sweeps down with the moor;
The river rushes into the wasteland.
Under the moon a heavenly mirror gyres
And clouds float, knotting an undersea palace.
Still thinking of the land and water of our home,
I see your sail depart for ten-thousand miles.

—Li Po (701–762)

III. Bitter Parting

At fifteen I was engaged to you
At twenty I was carried through the gate
Once I have entered your gate
I find you constantly away
In the morning I see you off
In the evening I see you off again
If I snap you another willow branch,
The tree will soon collapse.
I'd sooner be the dirt on the road
Where your horse hooves could rest.
I'd sooner be the branch of a tree
To serve as the wheel of your carriage.
Could I but move the high mountain
And block the horse's advance!

—Shao Yeh (late T'ang Dynasty)

JIM HARRISON

A Year's Changes

This nadir: the wet hole
in which a beast heaps twigs and bits
of hair, bark and tree skin,
both food and turds mix in the warm
dust its body makes.
In winter the dream of summer,
in summer the dream of sleep,
in spring feasting,
living dreams through the morning.
Fall, my cancer, pared to bone,
I lost my fur, my bite gone dull,
all edges, red and showing; now naked,
February painted with ice, preserve me
in wakefulness—I wait for the rain,
to see a red pine free of snow,
my body uncrabbed, unleashed,
my brain alive.

     * * *

In northern Manitoba
a man saw a great bald eagle—
hanging from its neck,
teeth locked in skin and feathers,
the bleached skull of a weasel.

     * * *

To sing not instinct or tact,
wisdom,
the song's full stop and death,
but audible things, things moving
at noon in full raw light;
a dog moving around
the tree with the shade—

shade and dog in motion—
alive at noon in full natural light.

* * *

This nightflower, the size of a cat's head—
now moist and sentient—
let it hang there in the dark;
bare beauty asking nothing of us,
if we could graft you to us,
so singular and married to the instant.
But now rest picked, a trillium
never to repeat yourself. Soon enough
you'll know dead air, bricf homage,
a sliver of glass in someone's brain.

* * *

Homesick for a dark, for clear black space
free of objects; to feel locked as wood
within a tree, a rock deep enough
in earth never to see the surface.

* * *

Snow. There's no earth left under it.
It's too cold to breathe.
Teeth ache, trees crack, the air is bluish.
My breath goes straight up.
This woods is so quiet
that if it weren't for the buffer of trees
I could hear everything on earth.

* * *

Only talk. Cloth after the pattern is cut,
discarded, spare wood barely kindling.
At night when the god in you trips,

hee-haws, barks and refuses to come
to tether. Stalk without quarry.
Yesterday I fired a rifle into the lake.

* * *

A cold spring dawn
near Parker Creek,
a doe bounding away through
shoulder-high fog
fairly floating,
soundless
as if she were running in a cloud.

* * *

That his death was disfigurement:
at impact when light passed
the cells yawned then froze in postures
unlike their former selves, teeth
stuck by the glue of their blood
to windshields, visors. And in the night,
a quiet snowy landscape, three bodies
slump, horribly rended.

* * *

Acacia Acidie Accipiter
flower boredom flight
gummy wet pale stemmed
barely above root level
and darkened by ferns;
but hawk
high now spots the cat he shot
and left there,
swings low

in narrowing circles,
feeds.

    * * *

My mouth stuffed up with snow,
nothing in me moves,
Earth nudges all things this month.
I've outgrown this shell
I found in a sea of ice—
its drunken convolutions—
something should call me to another life.

    * * *

Too cold for late May, snow flurries,
warblers tight in their trees, the air
with winter's clearness, dull
pearlish clear under clouds, clean
clear bite of wind, silver maple flexing
in the wind, wind rippling petals,
ripped from flowering crab,
pale pink against green firs, the body
chilled, blood unstirred, thick with frost:
body be snake,
self equal self to ground heat,
be wind cold, earth heated,
bend with tree, whip with grass,
move free clean and bright clear.

    * * *

Night draws on him until he's soft
and blackened, he waits for bones
sharp-edged as broken stone, rubble
in a deserted quarry, to defoliate,

come clean and bare
come clean and dry,
for salt,
he waits for salt.

* * *

In the dark I think of the fire,
how hot the shed was when it burned,
the layers of tar paper and dry pine,
the fruitlike billows and blue embers,
the exhausted smell as of a creature
beginning to stink when it has no more to eat.

* * *

The doe shot in the back
and just below the shoulder
has her heart and lungs blown out.
In the last crazed seconds she leaves
a circle of blood on the snow.
An hour later we eat
her still-warm liver for lunch,
fried in butter with onions.
In the evening we roast
her loins, and drink two gallons of red wine,
reeling drunken and yelling on the snow.
Jon Jackson will eat venison for month,
he has no job, food or money,
and his pump and well are frozen.

* * *

June, sun high, nearly straight above,
all green things in short weak shadow;
clipping acres of pine for someone's
Christmas, forearms sore with trimming,

itching with heat—
drawing boughs away from a trunk
a branch confused with the thick
ugliness of a hognose snake.

    * * *

Dogged days, dull, unflowering,
the mind petaled in cold wet dark;
outside the orange world is gray,
all things gray turned in upon
themselves in the globed eye of the seer—
gray seen.
But the orange world is orange to itself,
the war continues redly,
the moon is up in Asia,
the dark is only eight thousand miles deep.

    * * *

At the edge of the swamp a thorn apple tree
beneath which partridge feed on red berries,
and an elm tipped over in a storm
opening a circle of earth formerly closed,
huge elm roots in a watery place, bare,
wet, as if there were some lid to let
secrets out or a place where the ground
herself begins, then grows outward
to surround the earth; the hole, a black
pool of quiet water, the white roots
of undergrowth. It appears bottomless,
an oracle I should worship at; I want
some part of me to be lost in it and return
again from its darkness, changing the creature,
or return to draw me back to a home.

ADRIENNE RICH

from The Blue Ghazals

9/21/68

Violently asleep in the old house.
A clock stays awake all night ticking.

Turning, turning their bruised leaves
the trees stay awake all night in the wood.

Talk to me with your body through my dreams,
tell me what we are going through.

The walls of the room are muttering,
old trees, old Utopians, arguing with the wind.

To float like a dead man in a sea of dreams,
and half those dreams being dreamed by someone else.

Fifteen years of sleepwalking with you,
wading against the tide and with the tide.

9/23/68:i

One day of equinoctial light after another,
moving ourselves through gauzes & fissures of that light.

Early and late I come and set myself against you,
your phallic fist knocking blindly at my door.

The dew is beaded like mercury on the coarsened grass,
the web of the spider is heavy as if with sweat.

Everything is yielding toward a foregone conclusion,
only we are rash enough to go on changing our lives.

An Ashanti woman tilts the flattened basin on her head
to let the water slide downward: I am that woman & that water.

White and the River

I

I am my father.

I go out into the whiteness.
My skis slide their parallel
lines,
and poles alternate
their starprints.

I go to hunt some white thing,
some ptarmigan that lost all color
for this season,
I will hunt her home,
hang her by her feet in the cellar,
where she can spread
her white wings,
while I pull her snowfeathers
off
for the dark roast
she will become
on the white cloth

of my Sunday table,

—or some ermine,

regal white weasel
with the black tail tip,

I will catch
and kill,

strip the skin off
to reveal the smell.

Kings and queens are
little girl dreams.

—or a hare
will leap

shot.

II

And I am my brother.
I walk with my father
by the river.

We shall cross the river.
We know the ice is
thin.

I say:
"If you fall in
I will let you drown.

I will not pull you up.
I will push you
in."

And he looks at me,
and we walk, together,
out on the ice

that cracks,
but holds,
and cracks.

If he fell in
would he swim
underneath the ice,

groping for a place
where he would find
a breath,

and another,
to surface someplace,
further down river

where the current is harder
and ice cannot hold,
to return,

would he return
to swim in my dream?
—or sink

and lie on the bottom
as I lay
when I was four

and the boat had tipped over,
and my father found me
on the bottom of the river

and pulled me up
so that I can say:
"If you fall in
I will let you drown."

III

And I am my father,
and the boat has tipped over.

I dive for my son
again and
again,

until I see him lying
on the bottom of the river,

arms straight out
and eyes
looking up,

and I dive to his blue eyes
and pull the small body

through water to surface
air and
shore.

IV

And I am my mother,
I wash by the
river.

Boil the sheets
white,
and scrub at the
rugs.

The sun is warm.
It is good by
the river.

Rinse the clothes
clean
to blow dry
in the wind.

And my daughters call me.
"Run. Mamma.
Run.

The horse has kicked
brother.
The hoof in his
face."

The hoof in his face
while I wash by
the river.

The hoof in his face.

The hoof in his face.

V

Daughter, sister,
girl who picked
flowers,

(I wear a scar
on my face from
the hoof.)

marsh marigold,
the first by
the river,

"Why did you set
the furniture
on fire?"

and bunches of violets
brought home to
mother.

"Why did you lose
the nails and
the screws?"

I lifted the skulls of
cows and
oxen

observing, quite rightly,
that flowers grow
wilder

where bones
had been thrown
from the butchery shop.

VI

And I am my father,
and I stop,
pull an orange from the pocket
and peel it,
throw the peelings on the snow,

pick up my gun
and ski back home,
hang my white killing
on a hook in the cellar
where blood oranges lie

a crateful
of color
in winter.

December 1969

ALAN SOLDOFSKY

The North

> we come and go by the flares
> of campfires, full
> of ghosts with huge wounded hearts
> —John Haines

The snow here is
not deep, yet I imagine,
below the surface, that
generations of tiny foxes
are frozen to their
delicate skeletons.

Their fine bones have
partially turned to emeralds.
Their silver teeth glisten
in the arctic night. On
the wind come the
old voices, warning whales
of the dead. I too
stop and listen. My fingers
are cracked and almost
numb. Then the old ghosts
rise from the ice
like great gray birds.

Their eyes empty,
they carry their cold tales
to the frightened cities
of the south.

QUINCY TROUPE

White Weekend

April 5–8, 1968.

They deployed military troops
surrounded the White House
and on the steps of the Senate building
a soldier behind a machine gun

32,000 in Washington & Chicago
1900 in Baltimore Maryland
76 cities in flames on the landscape
and the bearer of peace
lying still in Atlanta

Lamentations! Lamentations! Lamentations!
Worldwide!
But in New York, on Wall Street
the stock market went up 18 points...

KEITH WILSON

Bridge Over the Pecos

—for my father, who knows
the River better than I do

There was this story about a railroad bridge.
Eleven men died, fell into the wet concrete pillars,
were left there, stone men holding up the ties
spikes, shining rails

        Others say white men
killed them. They were black, story goes, one
for each pillar, for luck, for the blood
that binds stone and locks it into place.

Later, a switching engine fell when the roadbed
shifted, it tumbled steaming, its bright wheels
whirling suns, fell in heavy black arc
into quicksand

        Crew, engine and all sank beneath
the greysilver sands and are down there yet, dead
hand near the throttle

        Sun, rising over the Pecos, wind
wild in the cedar brakes, rabbits catching the scent
of foxes on their twitching noses, river run muddy
clouding the old stories, blurring the faces...
How many deaths it takes to move a people across
a land

        Bridge, dead black marching pillars.
The bronze sun, Indian songs beside, quiet river.

The New Mexican

—for Frank Waters who created New Mexican literature,
in warm and affectionate memory

From one of the draws, out of a mountain
across plains heavy with grass or dry
bleached and cracked by the sun

                    He came
rifle easy in his hand, a hunting dogtrot
in his heart, brain singing with the hunt
the need for a kill

          Old mountain men, born
and raised for the power of their hands & arms
valuing themselves little past those physical
strengths, and what survival finally cost them
when the necessities, time, disappeared
with the game

Old men sitting on porches or scratching out
gardens, their blue black brown green eyes
cutting out a trail that now only hawks
dare follow

        Out of the North come the snows
falling on storebought windows. Old men get
laid into frozen earth, their big hands
holding scars like lilies the coming Springs
may never bear again . . . .

E.G. BURROWS

Year's End (1968)

1.

Hare tracks go straight
over the snow hill. Stop. Double
print of owl wings spread

at the end of the hare's trail each
feather's mark like the pressed veins
of a leaf in silence in granite

and only the grey swatch of fur
and the red hardly visible blemish
of blood where the claw struck.

Sun tilts off the ridge,
lies heavily south hull down
like a burning freighter, pulls

a long scrawl of shadow from each
crater's rim. I tower above them
with the astronauts' *frisson.*

The signs are callous. Discreet
winds dab absorbent gusts
of mind-thickening snow to wipe

the world empty again or until
a thrust of flowers thaws
violence to a quibble.

2.

The black children of Biafra
spit metal. Skies split
with the same cradle croon
under Mekong thatch.

In cold theaters, teams
of gauze-mouthed men worry
among the ribs of the dead
for a matching heart.

The bank has bloodily failed.
I grope in the dark for a heart
quiet on a balcony in Memphis,
unfathomed off the Canaries

in a boat of steel, sealed
in the company's No. 9 shaft,
on the floor of a hotel pantry,
a heart stiff with the blows

of Chicago thugs. I touch
the cold side of a waste rock in the high
sierras of space. I count
the slow coin in my wrist.

3.

La sangre de nuestros
campaneros: curriculum
of the exclamatory young.
Book of the streets.
Descent of the red laurel.
A library of wounds.

Arrives the sorefooted
marathon, breath gnashing
in the thin military air.
Runners stretch toward the gun.
The instruction begins
along the world's boulevards:

plaza del toro,
commedia of the arts
in the snarl of lean dogs,
science a chemical spray
against the rabid truth.
O the seminars of power!

After the death of thirty-three
it was all Games.
After the black fists a rain
of anthems and gold chains,
the True Olive in a box.

AMEEN ALWAN

Signs at Ft. Polk, La.

this area

closed
to deer hunting

this season

for protection
of US troops

training

for Vietnam
warfare

JOHN CALVIN REZMERSKI

The Radio Says Something About Hog Cholera and the Battle at Dak To (I Don't Know Any Pigs but I Remember What We All Remember, That Animals Were Gods Before Men)

Children go through life like meteors.
Every one changes more air to ash.
So little time to fret about the price of pork,
not much chance to burn candles in front of statues.
Sometimes you reach out and burn your hand on a child.
Listen to the birds again, believe them.
The sky is really falling this time.

A crow,

    above the rooftops,
    black against a sky almost white.

    A man stands on the other side of the street
    with his dog, both looking at it

    flying through two
       —or if the woman in the window sees it—

    through three brains
    up there with the crow & me

    altogether five brains
    flying

DAVE KELLY

Dance of the Eagle

They always led their captive
to the same place, a flat runway
at the top of one of their hills
and stripped him there. It was a
death reserved for only the great
warriors among their enemies.
With the wind screaming around
them, they stood the man on his
feet and two of them held him
there. Then one would take the
sharpest knife and move behind the
three of them. The holders pulled
his arms out straight and the
man with the knife would slit a
long wedge down the back on each
side by the shoulder bone, always
careful not to cut the heart.
When the back was sliced open
on both sides, the man with the
knife would drop the knife and
plunge a hand into each hole
while the other two looked deep
into their prisoner's face for
a certain look of readiness in
the eyes. At a nod from one, the
knifer would pull both hands deft-
ly from the slits. Each hand held
a lung and yanked it from its

socket. The two men dropped their
victim's arms and he would always
run straight down the track, his
elbows pushing behind him to fill
the gaps in his back. They called
them wings. They called the sound
that whistled out his wounds and
mouth the eagle's song. When he
fell they rolled his body down
the hill. The lungs they cooked
and fed to their dogs at night.

The Dead Shall Be Raised Incorruptible

1

A piece of flesh gives off
smoke in the field—

carrion,
caput mortuum,
orts,
pelf,
fenks,
sordes,
gurry dumped from hospital trashcans.

Lieutenant!
This corpse will not stop burning!

2

"That you, Captain? Sure,
sure I remember—I still hear you
lecturing at me on the intercom, *Keep your guns up, Burnsie!*
and then screaming, *Stop shooting, for crissake, Burnsie,*
those are friendlies! But crissake, Captain,
I'd already started, burst
after burst, little black pajamas jumping
and falling...and remember that pilot
who'd bailed out over the North,
how I shredded him down to catgut on his strings?
one of his slant eyes, a piece
of his smile, sail past me
every night right after the sleeping pill...

"It was only
that I loved the *sound*
of them, I guess I just loved
the *feel* of them sparkin' off my hands..."

3

On the television screen:

Do you have a body that sweats?
Sweat that has odor?
False teeth clanging into your breakfast?
Case of the dread?
Headache so perpetual it may outlive you?
Armpits that sprout hair?
Piles so huge you don't need a chair to sit at table?

We shall not all sleep, but we shall be changed.

4

In the Twentieth Century of my trespass on earth,
having exterminated one billion heathens,
heretics, Jews, Moslems, witches, mystical seekers,
black men, Asians, and white Christian brothers,
every one of them for his own good,

a whole continent of red men for living in unnatural
    community
and at the same time having relations with the land,
one billion species of animals for being sub-human,

and ready to take on the bloodthirsty creatures from the
  other planets,
I, Christian man, groan out this testament of my last will.

I give my blood fifty parts polystyrene,
twenty-five parts benzene, twenty-five parts good old gasoline,
to the last bomber pilot aloft, that there shall be one acre
in the dull world where the kissing flower may bloom,
which kisses you so long your bones explode under its lips.

My tongue goes to the Secretary of the Dead
to tell the corpses, "I'm sorry, fellows,
the killing was just one of those things
difficult to pre-visualize—like a cow,
say, getting hit by lightning."

My stomach, which has digested
four hundred treaties giving the Indians
eternal right to their land, I give to the Indians;
as well as my lungs which have spent four hundred years
sucking earnestly on peace pipes.

My soul I leave to the bee
that he may sting it and die, my brain
to the fly, his back the hysterical green color of slime,
that he may suck on it and die, my flesh to the advertising man,
the anti-prostitute, who loathes human flesh for money.

I assign my crooked backbone
to the dice maker, to chop up into dice,
for casting lots as to who shall see his own blood

on his shirt front and who his brother's,
for the race isn't to the swift but to the crooked.

To the last man surviving on earth
I give my eyelids worn out by fear, to wear
in his long nights of radiation and silence,
so that his eyes can't close, for regret
is like tears seeping through closed eyelids.

I give the emptiness my hand: the little finger picks no
    more noses,
slag clings to the black stick of the ring finger,
a bit of flame jets from the tip of the fuck-you finger,
the first finger accuses the heart, which has vanished,
on the thumb stump wisps of smoke ask a ride into the
    emptiness.

In the Twentieth Century of my nightmare
on earth, I swear on my chromium testicles
to this testament
and last will
of my iron will, my fear of love, my itch for money, and my
    madness.

5

In the ditch
snakes crawl cool paths
over the rotted thigh, the toe bones
twitch in the smell of burnt rubber,
the belly

opens like a poison nightflower,
the tongue has evaporated,
the nostril
hairs sprinkle themselves with yellowish-white dust,
the five flames at the end
of each hand have gone out, a mosquito
sips a last meal from this plate of serenity.

And the fly,
the last nightmare, hatches himself.

6

I ran
my neck broken I ran
holding my head up with both hands I ran
thinking the flames
the flames may burn the oboe
but listen buddy boy they can't touch the notes!

7

A few bones
lie about in the smoke of bones.

Membranes,
effigies pressed into grass,
mummy windings,
desquamations,
sags incinerated mattresses gave back to the world,

memories left in mirrors on whorehouse ceilings,
angel's wings
flagged down into the snows of yesteryear,

kneel
on the scorched earth
in the shapes of men and animals:

do not let this last hour pass,
do not remove this last, poison cup from our lips.

And a wind holding
the cries of love-making from all our nights and days
moves among the stones, hunting
for two twined skeletons to blow its last cry across.

Lieutenant!
This corpse will not stop burning!

GEORGE QUASHA

Total Immersion in the Tank at Allapattah Baptist Church

1.

I watched them going down,
drowning in God's water,
and I found myself wanting
only to drown in
her, the woman waiting across the water,
14 feet from my swollen manhood
worming at, trying to grow thru,
my white gown. One
by one, before me, they were reborn
sputtering holy water with hair caught in their teeth.
I was not. I was the same. I wanted
the woman but it was God
who had her. He shoved her into my holiness and
took her for Himself. I'm a better man for it,
I thought, bending to hide my rising
sin from the eyes of God who put it
there. I held it against Him
that my longing to enter the holy place
should end where it began. Outside and
hovering on the rim of the great pool,
the body whining with originality
balanced by an aimless prick

2.

It was she who went down
first, yielding herself
from the ladies' side.
When would she come
back, was all I was thinking
but the preacher holding tight her pure white shield
brought her forth from the water
made flesh, translucent
and shaped like skipping mountains
—I couldn't help it, I felt the dark cave
drawing me forward, and my own turn came and entered
the cool of God's mouth, I was struggling hard
to drown, I was leaning backwards to,
his arm choked me as He came in my nose, and
I spit Him out, she was gone
and there was only me
coming up

Frog Hollow
12/4/69

Smokey the Bear Sutra

Once in the Jurassic, about 150 million years ago,
the Great Sun Buddha in this corner of the Infinite
Void gave a great Discourse to all the assembled elements
and energies: to the standing beings, the walking beings,
the flying beings, and the sitting beings—even grasses,
to the number of thirteen billion, each one born from a
seed, were assembled there: a Discourse concerning
Enlightenment on the planet Earth.

"In some future time, there will be a continent called
America. It will have great centers of power called
such as Pyramid Lake, Walden Pond, Mt. Rainier, Big Sur,
Everglades, and so forth; and powerful nerves and channels
such as Columbia River, Mississippi River, and Grand Canyon.
The human race in that era will get into troubles all over
its head, and practically wreck everything in spite of
its own strong intelligent Buddha-nature."

"The twisting strata of the great mountains and the pulsings
of great volcanoes are my love burning deep in the earth.
My obstinate compassion is schist and basalt and
granite, to be mountains, to bring down the rain. In that
future American Era I shall enter a new form: to cure
the world of loveless knowledge that seeks with blind hunger;
and mindless rage eating food that will not fill it."

And he showed himself in his true form of

SMOKEY THE BEAR.

A handsome smokey-colored brown bear standing on his
hind legs, showing that he is aroused and watchful.

Bearing in his right paw the Shovel that digs to the
truth beneath appearances; cuts the roots of useless attach-
ments, and flings damp sand on the fires of greed and war;

His left paw in the Mudra of Comradely Display—
indicating that all creatures have the full right to live to their
limits and that deer, rabbits, chipmunks, snakes, dandelions,
and lizards all grow in the realm of the Dharma;

Wearing the blue work overalls symbolic of slaves and
laborers, the countless men oppressed by civilization
that claims to save but only destroys;

Wearing the broad-brimmed hat of the West, symbolic of
the forces that guard the Wilderness, which is the Natural
State of the Dharma and the True Path of man on earth;
all true paths lead through mountains—

With a halo of smoke and flame behind, the forest fires
of the kali-yuga, fires caused by the stupidity of those
who think things can be gained and lost whereas in truth all
is contained vast and free in the Blue Sky and Green Earth
of One Mind;

Round-bellied to show his kind nature and that the great
earth has food enough for everyone who loves her and trusts
her;

Trampling underfoot wasteful freeways and needless
suburbs; smashing the worms of capitalism and totalitarianism;

Indicating the Task: his followers, becoming free of cars,
houses, canned food, universities, and shoes, master the
Three Mysteries of their own Body, Speech, and Mind; and
fearlessly chop down the rotten trees and prune out the
sick limbs of this country America and then burn the leftover
trash.

Wrathful but Calm, Austere but Comic, Smokey the Bear will
Illuminate those who would help him; but for those who would
hinder or slander him,

HE WILL PUT THEM OUT.

Thus his great Mantra:

Namah samanta vajranam chanda maharoshana
Sphataya hum traka ham mam

"I DEDICATE MYSELF TO THE UNIVERSAL DIAMOND
BE THIS RAGING FURY DESTROYED"

And he will protect those who love woods and rivers,
Gods and animals, hobos and madmen, prisoners and sick
people, musicians, playful women, and hopeful children;

And if anyone is threatened by advertising, air pollution,
or the police, they should chant SMOKEY THE BEAR'S
WAR SPELL:

DROWN THEIR BUTTS
CRUSH THEIR BUTTS
DROWN THEIR BUTTS
CRUSH THEIR BUTTS

And SMOKEY THE BEAR will surely appear to put the enemy
out with his vajra-shovel.

Now those who recite this Sutra and then try to put it in
    practice will accumulate merit as countless as the sands
    of Arizona and Nevada,
Will help save the planet Earth from total oil slick,
Will enter the age of harmony of man and nature,
Will win the tender love and caresses of men, women, and
    beasts,
Will always have ripe blackberries to eat and a sunny spot
    under a pine tree to sit at,

AND IN THE END WILL WIN HIGHEST PERFECT ENLIGHTENMENT.

    thus have we heard.

(may be reproduced free forever)

TU FU

five translations by Morgan Gibson

Gazing at the Great Peak

What's this godly mountain like?
Its green is endless through Ch'i and Lu.
Its beauty was gathered by the Creator.
It splits dawn from darkness, yang from yin.
Clouds breed in layers around my heaving chest.
Returning birds enter my bursting eyes.
I must reach the top
To see, all at once, many mountains grown small.

Moonlit Night

Tonight in Fu-chou, moonlight:
Lonely, my wife watches.
I miss my sons and daughters far away.
They don't understand
   don't remember me in Ch'ang-an.
Mist dampens the cloud of my wife's sweet hair.
Moonlight chills her jade-white arms.
When will we lean against curtains together?
When will our shining tears dry?

Remembering My Brothers In a Moonlit Night

Garrison drums stop travel.
The honking of a lonely goose
        announces autumn on the frontier.
From this night on, the dew will be white.
The same moon shines on my home.
All my brothers are scattered.
I have no family:
        are they dead or alive?
Letters sent never arrive
because fighting has not ended.

Spring View

If the State falls, mountains and rivers remain.
Spring in the city: thick grass and trees.
Flowers shed tears for these chaotic times.
Birds startle the heart, hating separation.
War beacons have burned for three months.
A letter from home would be worth ten thousand dollars.
I've scratched my hair so short
It won't be enough for a hatpin!

Ballad of Army Carts

Rumbling carts rambling
horses whinnying
draftees have bows and arrows at the waist.
Fathers and mothers, wives and children run to see them off
near the Hsien-yang Bridge, invisible in dust
yanking uniforms, stamping feet, standing in the way, crying.
Crying bombards the cloudy sky.
Somebody passing asks draftees
and draftees reply: "We're always moving out.
Some of us were fifteen when we guarded the northern river.
Now at forty we're heading west to army farms.
When we left as kids the village chief had to tie our turbans.
Coming back white haired we have to serve on the frontier.
On the frontier blood flows like seawater
but the Emperor's dreams of conquest haven't ended.
Sir, haven't you heard that in two hundred countries of Han
        east of the mountains
briars and thorns cover thousands of villages and hamlets?
Strong wives take up hoe and plough
but no crops grow east or west.
Ch'in soldiers can fight hard
but are driven like dogs or chickens.
Though you have asked, sir
draftees don't dare to speak out.
This winter, for instance
the Kuan-hsi troops aren't demobilized.
Governors push for land taxes.
Land taxes!—where will they come from?

You'd better believe it's bad to bear a son:
better have a daughter.
If a daughter, she can marry a neighbor.
If a son, he'll lie in grass, unburied.
Sir, don't you see on shores of the Blue Sea
white bones lying for ages, ungathered?
New ghosts complain, old ghosts wail:
from the grey rainy sky their voices twitter."

A War Story

WHEN RHONDA WAS SEVENTEEN she switched to Kent cigarettes. Rory smoked Kents and he wanted her to smoke them too. Before Rory and the Kents, she had smoked Camels because her first steady, Buck, smoked Camels.

Five years later she was watching television with her mother one night when a new commercial came on. A sharp-faced, cold but handsome man wearing very mysterious-looking wraparound sunglasses lit a cigarette. He inhaled, sharp-lipped—staring through the black glasses straight at Rhonda—and as he exhaled the smoke out the corner of his mouth, Rhonda and her mother were informed that latest government figures showed that Silva Thins were lowest in nicotine and tars of all 100s.

She fell in love with the pale, cruel-faced man who smoked Silva Thins. In later commercials for the same cigarette, the man in the sunglasses snatched his Silva Thins from beautiful girls who tried to steal them from him. Rhonda liked that. It gave her a strange little ache. She shifted her eyes to the gilt-framed photograph of Rory on the television set: he was wearing his dress uniform and white hat. When she thought about other men, she immediately thought about Rory. She knew she should be ashamed of herself for thinking about other men while Rory was in Vietnam. But she got used to being ashamed of herself, and before long it didn't bother her very much to think about, say, the red-headed carry-out boy at Kroger's, or Mr. Tyler next door, even though he was fifty or sixty years old.

Rhonda spent her time until Rory got back by running around with Vicki. She and Vicki had been best friends in high school. Vicki had got married and then she and her husband got a divorce after a couple of years. Rhonda and Vicki and some of her other girl friends from high school went horseback-riding and they went to the beach together when they could. Most of them were married too, and most of them had changed a great deal since they got married. And they knew it. It amazed them. Vicki one time told Rhonda that since she had been married and divorced she had learned more about life than in all the rest of her life put together, and what she had learned she didn't especially like.

Now and then she and the girls played bridge in the afternoons and drank martinis, and sometimes they just went to the Sump late in the afternoons and drank beer, and then the other girls' husbands would come after they got off work, and then sometimes they would all of them go on drinking beer until the Sump closed and then go to someone's house for a party.

Rhonda met Kim that way. And Charlie Chan, and an older guy named Cousin. He interested her most. He was short and stocky and bald-headed except around the edges. In a way he reminded her of the pictures of her father—except Cousin was nice and sympathetic, and her father hadn't seen her or written her in years. Cousin sympathized with her and told her he knew what it was like for a fellow to be off at war with a young wife waiting at home, because he had been in World War Two. He had been in Europe fighting while his wife was at home. It didn't bother him now, he said, striking a kitchen match under his thumbnail and lighting her cigarette, but it turned out later that while he was off fighting in Europe, his wife was sleeping with a different man every night. It had been hard for him to understand why she had done it, he said. But now that he was older, he said—grinning and running his hand over his bald head—he understood it very clearly. It was a matter of being alive, he said. There are people right this minute somewhere dying—right now! He snapped his thick fingers. But there are lots of others who are still alive. He smiled. Very much alive.

Rhonda laughed. But then she started crying. She was ashamed that it was so easy for her to be alive. "Does that make sense?" she asked Cousin, as she took his handkerchief.

Cousin drove her home and parked with her in the shadows of the big elm trees in front of her mother's house.

And it was the next night she was watching television with her mother and she saw the brutal, pale-faced man in the commercial for Silva Thins. She would have got up right then and there and gone out and bought a pack of them, but she had promised her mother she would stay home for a change. And she would have gone down to the filling station on the corner and telephoned Cousin, if she had known his number or where he lived, or if she had even known his real name, for she knew Cousin wasn't really his name. It was just the name he used when he was on the make.

*

The day she smoked her first pack of Silva Thins she got up at eight, when her mother got up. She ate a big breakfast. (Rory had always kidded her about how much she ate in the mornings. He kidded her and said that she ate so much for breakfast because she worked so hard at night.) While her mother cleaned the house, Rhonda went out onto the patio and started writing her letter to Rory.

For a while she had been worried she would have trouble writing to him. Especially yesterday. She was hungover and all she could do was sit, holding herself back from crying, looking at Rory's photograph, and thinking about what she had let Cousin do.

But this morning when she got up she felt like a million dollars and she knew she wouldn't have any trouble writing to Rory.

She started the letter the same way she did all the others, "My Dearest Darling Rory," and it just went on from there. She made a joke in the letter about why she hadn't written yesterday. She told him when he came back he would have to get mad at Vicki because she said Vicki had got crocked and that Rhonda had got just a little squacked, and she had felt so bad yesterday morning she just couldn't manage to write.

She wrote several pages of the letter and by then the sun was up over the trees and she went upstairs to her room and put on her yellow bikini and got her beach towel. Her mother was coming out of the kitchen as she was going back out onto the patio. "Is it today you're going to Debbie's tea? Do you have your oil?"

"Yes. No."

"I'll bring it out."

On the patio she tossed the stationery box and beach towel onto a plastic lawn chair. She walked out to the little shed to get the air mattress. She walked slowly, concentrating on her hips, and as she walked she lifted her arms and patted her fingertips at the back of her neck for any loose hairs. She brought the air mattress and little foot pump out of the shed and pumped it up. As she carried it back to the patio, she glanced over at Mr. Tyler's next door. She saw a curtain move.

She spread the towel on the air mattress and lay down on her stomach. "Here I am again," she wrote, noticing her handwriting had changed from when she interrupted her letter. Now the words were bigger, freer. She went on with the letter, telling Rory about one of the television shows she had seen last night. After a while her mother came out with a tray.

"I think while you're at that tea this afternoon I'm going to go over and see Paula Burns. I'll call her a little later and see if she's going to be home and... Want me to go ahead and put this on your back?"

"Yes."

Her mother untied the bra string in back and squirted some oil on Rhonda's back. She began to slowly, gently smooth on the oil, and she went on talking, and Rhonda went on writing her letter to Rory.

"Do the back of my legs."

"All right," and she went on talking and then stopped and Rhonda felt the little pain again. "You've got a little bruise right...*there*. Do you feel that?"

"Yes." She kept writing.

Only a thumbprint of the bruise showed beneath the tight edge of the bikini. "How did you get that?"

"Getting in Vicki's M.G."

And at the same time she mentioned Vicki and her M.G. in her letter to Rory, inventing a story about how she and Vicki went shopping out at the new Northland Center.

Her mother brought out some wine coolers around eleven, and Rhonda finished her letter to Rory. Then she lay on her back for a long time, the drink making her seem very weak and helpless, the sun's victim, and she dozed off. The sun pressed itself against her, and though she wasn't dreaming, she made a fantasy in which Rory was home and they were down at the beach and the beach was deserted and she put her arms around his legs and held him, looking up at him, and they took their swimming suits off and lay down in the sand, the sun burned into her, and she turned her head in the sand and saw up among the weeds back from the beach the faces of people, many people, watching her and Rory.

She and her mother had lunch, and her mother nagged her some about her constipation problem and made her eat some prunes and made her promise she would drink a cup of warm water or a cup of Sanka before she went to bed. That would help.

Rhonda went upstairs and dressed, and when she left for the tea (though the tea wasn't until four o'clock), she left the house with the feeling that she was forgetting something. She hadn't driven two blocks before she remembered it was Rory's letter. She stopped her car to make a u-turn and go back for it, but she didn't turn the car around but drove on. Her mother would mail it for her. She hoped her mother would remember to send it air mail.

*

She drove out to the Northland Shopping Center, went into some of the small shops, and walked through several of the big stores. Then she drove on out to a little resort town where there was an open market. She strolled around for a while and then went to a sidewalk café. She wanted a Coke, but for her mother's sake she ordered a cup of coffee.

She still had the weak, sun-drained feeling she had got that morning. Maybe it was from yesterday's hangover. And she didn't like to admit it, but her mother was right—she was a little constipated. She looked across the café at a large mirror and she saw that even if she didn't feel good, she still looked good. She was, in fact, beautiful. And Rhonda didn't feel she was vain. She was realistic. It was a good idea to be realistic about who you are and what you want to do with yourself.

She was being watched. A man wearing a white turtleneck sweater and a navy blue blazer was sitting between her and the mirror. He probably thought she was looking at him. He was thirty-five or forty, not very good-looking, though he had a rough, hairy kind of good looks. He had big thick hands.

The coffee... the sun... her constipation... the constant worrying about Rory over there with all that danger... the strange feeling that all this was happening somewhere else, in some place she had never seen before, like in a foreign country and she wasn't Rhonda... She had the feeling that all the familiar things around her were putting on costumes right before her eyes and that there was nothing for her to do but to watch everything happen, watch it all go flying by as if she were watching the Huntley-Brinkley show and believing, fearing that at any moment she would see Rory right there on the television screen lying on the ground crying with a hole in him.

The man came over to her table and asked if he could join her.

She looked at him with no expression.

He said his name was Herb. She said nothing, and he told a joke about his name being Herb. He laughed hard, his eyes wrinkling up tightly, his thick hard-white teeth showing.

"Would you buy me a pack of Silva Thins?" Rhonda said. She didn't know why she said it.

He hesitated, his hardy grin shifting very slightly to a squint that was close to a frown, but he was a man who was quick at sensing signals, and he said, "Sure. Sure. You bet. Be right back," and he got up and went into the café, glancing over his shoulder out at her to see she wasn't going to slip away. He came out again, paused at the table, "They don't have them here. Be right back. Don't run away. Okay?"

She still could get no expression in her face, and his face bordered between a muscular, hard smile, and a scowl.

She watched him go down the sidewalk to another restaurant. He came out almost immediately, didn't look back at the sidewalk café, but hurried up the street in the other direction to a drugstore. He was longer coming out, but when he did he held up something in his hand, and he hurried back, his head down, his shoulders squared.

"Here," he said, setting the package of cigarettes on their end beside her coffee cup. Silva Thins. "How's that?"

She smiled his direction.

*

Her mother stopped talking to her. Then a few days later she tried talking to her again, tried reasoning with her. She threatened Rhonda with the family doctor. Then she stopped talking to her again. When she talked to her again she threatened to take her to see Rory's mother and father.

And the time rushed by free of its usual slow meaning, and it was exciting and horrible. Her mother watched her closely. Rhonda let her have serious conversations with her, and Rhonda sometimes cried and made promises. Her mother had their minister out and Rhonda cried and satisfied him and her mother, and that night she went out again.

Finally her mother blurted out one morning as Rhonda sat at the breakfast table choking down toast and black coffee, her body and her mind aching, that she thought Rhonda was becoming depressed about being away from Rory for so long.

Rhonda cried, her mother cried, and in the middle of it Rhonda had to jump up and run to the bathroom. Her mother came and stood in the door, wiping her eyes with a Kleenex, and commented that at least Rhonda's constipation was better.

Then Rhonda started crying when she was alone. Once when she was waiting in a motel room for an old high school friend,

Bill Barker, she started crying with desperation. It was a frenzy of crying that was so violent and overpowering that there was a real, awful thrill in it, and she slowly took her clothes off and lay with her legs apart, crying, hating herself and loving herself, staring up at the ceiling.

And a few days later she had cried so hard while she was driving to meet an older man named Wayne, that she was afraid—and thrilled with the fear—that she would have an accident. It was raining and the windshield was wet as if with her tears, and she drove faster and she rolled down the window and breathed the rain.

But she didn't cry when she got a long-distance telephone call from a Marine captain in San Diego who told her that her husband, Lance Corporal Rory Roberts, had been wounded in action in Vietnam. He told her that in a few hours she and the corporal's parents would be contacted by a Marine Corps representative who would make arrangements for them to be flown to Guam to the hospital where Rory would be taken as soon as he could be removed from Tan Sanut.

When Rhonda and Mrs. Roberts went to Guam, they were given a room in the big, glaring white hospital, and a Marine doctor gave them sedatives. A nurse was with them every now and then for the two days prior to Rory's arrival at the hospital. They had been prepared for his condition when he came.

Rory had stepped on a claymore landmine. He had been badly wounded. The doctors didn't know if he could survive. If he did, the doctors didn't know if he could adjust to the way his life would be changed.

Mrs. Roberts repeated perhaps a hundred times a day that she was numb. Rhonda said she was numb too. Saying they were numb helped more than the sedatives.

Then Rory was brought to the hospital. They couldn't see him for four days, then five. But knowing he was there, somewhere in that big white hospital, helped. Mrs. Roberts repeatedly said it helped. Rhonda also believed it helped.

Then they were allowed to see him. Rhonda first, for five minutes. Then Mrs. Roberts.

They were no longer numb. And the sedatives didn't seem to work. Mrs. Roberts was hysterical. Rhonda sat in her bed and smoked cigarettes, staring at her little travel alarm. Then she started crying. The crying carried her into a deeper crying which had more meaning than any crying she had ever done before. It went on and on, she had no control over it, it felt as if she were turning herself wrong side out, and still it came.

*

Two months later she was in Rory's room in the big Navy hospital in San Diego and they were listening to the transistor on the windowsill beside the bed. The room was white and light green—a bright, pleasant room that faced north. Rory's father had hung glass wind chimes in front of the window, and they tinkled in the gentle breeze.

Rory licked his lips.

"Like a cigarette, Rory?"

He moved his head.

She lit a Kent for him and put it between his lips. With his tongue, he moved it over to the corner of his mouth, and inhaled deeply. He exhaled the smoke slowly from his nostrils.

On the transistor The Doors sang "Light My Fire." She hummed along softly. She stared at his eye sockets. They were brown.

In the corridor a woman laughed, there was a broken conversation, then more laughter.

"Ashes," Rhonda said and slowly reached across him and held the cigarette until he carefully backed his lips from around it. "There," she said. She flicked the ashes into the white ceramic USMC ash tray on the bedside table. She put the cigarette back between his lips.

He finished the cigarette and then there was the news on the radio. They listened to the news and then there was more music. The Beatles sang "Hello Goodbye," one of Rory's favorites. Rhonda thought she heard him humming it.

"I guess I'll go eat lunch," she said.

"Okay."

"It's about one o'clock."

He nodded his head.

"Mom and I'll be back this afternoon. Your dad said he was going to see about getting you a different room so that you can get some sun. So I don't know if he'll be here until later this afternoon or not."

"He doesn't have to do that."

"I know it but he wants to. Let him do it, Rory. He wants to."

"I don't want him making any trouble for them."

"He won't. It just worries him the sun doesn't come in here."

Rory was silent. He had a strange way of going off, right in the middle of a conversation. He would just stop, and whoever was in the room would look at him and be afraid for a moment or two.

"So I'll see you later this afternoon," Rhonda said.

He nodded his head slightly.

Rhonda went over to the window and got the transistor, turned it off, and put it in the drawer of the bedside table.

Then she leaned over the narrow bed. She closed her eyes and kissed his lips gently, barely touching them.

She lifted her head slightly. She felt his breath on her lips. "Rory," she whispered, but the name didn't form completely. He didn't respond.

She kissed him again, as lightly as before, but she left her mouth against his.

Slowly, carefully, she put her arm under his neck. Very slowly she sat on the side of the bed and then lay down beside him. "Does that hurt?" she whispered. He said nothing. "I'm not hurting you am I, Rory?"

"No," he whispered.

She leaned her face against him, rubbing his cheek with her nose and lips.

For a long time she lay there, her eyes closed, and then she sat up on the side of the bed. She felt very heavy, as if she were full, bloated. She took off her blouse and stared at the door of the narrow white room. She took off her bra and stood up and took off her shoes, hose and her skirt, slip, and panties. She stood beside the bed looking by the wind chimes and out the window. She lay down again beside him, and she put her arm gently under his neck again and her other arm across his chest and she held him, her eyes closed, breathing deeply, and then she slowly pushed the sheet down his chest, but not down to his stomach. "Rory," she whispered. He didn't move. She slowly lifted herself on her elbow and leaned over him, but lightly, not pressing down on him. She kissed his cheeks and his forehead and his nose and lips. She spread her legs and slowly, carefully, she straddled his stomach, above where his hips should have been, and she remained there, not moving, her eyes shut tight, her teeth clenched. Not looking, she reached out to the left side and pushed down the sheet, lifting her left knee. She pushed it down on the right side, but it became hung on something and she opened her eyes and saw it was twisted around the catheter tube that ran into his stomach. She untangled the sheet from the rubber tube and pushed the sheet down the rest of the way.

Then she hovered over him, both hands under his head, her cheek against his, her breasts pressing lightly against his chest.

Slowly she lowered herself, her legs spreading wider, until she touched an uneven fringe of skin.

After a while, she got up. She kept her eyes closed as she pulled the sheet up onto his chest. She sat on the side of the bed, staring straight ahead, and after a while she reached over to her purse on the bedside table and got a cigarette and lit it.

Then she put on her clothes. She didn't say anything to him, but walked out of the room.

Outside the hospital there were people. Everywhere she looked there were people, thousands of them.

She sat in her car a moment, looking at the street in front of the hospital. Cars and people. She looked at them as they drove by. Their faces were blank, serious.

She started her car and drove across the lot to the exit. She watched the fast-moving traffic, waiting for a chance to pull into the street. When she saw her chance, she tromped the accelerator and she was in the traffic, moving fast, alert, her eyes open wide.

JAMES TATE

Wait for Me

A dream of life a dream of birth
a dream of moving
from one world into another

All night dismantling the synapses
unplugging the veins and arteries...

Hello I am a cake of soap
dissolving in a warm bath

A train with no windows and no doors
a lover with no eyes for his mask
—inside is the speed of life.

Who can doubt the words of it
each letter written is obsolete
before it finds its friend

Our life is shorter now
full of chaotic numbers
which never complete a day

It will be the same
as it has always been
and you are right to pack

your heart in ice
if you believe this.

Song

The girl with the beautiful face
is gathering olives.
The wind, lover of towers,
is taking her by the waist.

Four riders passed
on Andalusian ponies,
wearing blue and green,
wearing long dark capes.
"Come to Cordoba, maid."
The girl ignores them.

Three young bullfighters passed,
with slender waists,
wearing orange suits
and swords of antique silver.
"Come to Seville, maid."
The girl ignores them.

When early evening became
purple, with a scattered light,
a youth passed bringing
roses and myrtle of the moon.
"Come to Granada, maid."
But the girl ignores him.

The girl with the beautiful face
goes on gathering olives,
the gray arm of the wind
winding around her waist.

translated by James Tipton

JAMES WELCH

Gravely

We watched her go the way she came,
unenvied, wild—cold as last spring rain.
Mule deer browsed her garden down
to labored earth, seed and clean carrots.

Dusk is never easy, yet she took it
like her plastic saint, grandly, the day
we cut those morning glories down
and divvied up her odds and ends.

Daughters burned sheets the following Monday.
All over God's city, the high white stars
welcomed her the way she'd planned: A chilly
satellite ringing round the great malicious moon.

BARBARA DRAKE

She Dreams Herself Titanic

She dreams herself titanic
like the boat
that could not sink
but did not float,
and in her ears
what he lusts for,
crystal chandeliers.
Again the jewelled
iceberg tears,
again the waters pour,
again the voice of ice—
I'll ride you
to the velvet floor.
She wakes at dawn,
nine hundred miles from shore,
submerged and calm.

LOUIS SIMPSON

Port Jefferson

My whole life coming to this place,
and understanding it better
maybe for having been born
offshore, and at an early age
left to my own support...

I have come where sea and wind,
wave and leaf, are one sighing,
where the house strains at an anchor
and the salt-rose clings and clambers
on the humorous grave.

This is the place, Camerado,
that hides the sea-bird's nest.
When the wind flattens the grass it
shines, and there are stones
smoothed by the waves that are a joy to hold.

The Psyche of Riverside Drive

The wind was packed with cold.
He pushed against it, over to the Drive
and down a block—watching his step
so as not to slip in the icy slush.

He went through the ritual of entering a building—
speaking on the intercom, the buzzing
and opening of the second door.
He trod the path worn in the carpet
from the entrance to the elevator.

On the right the girl in marble,
Psyche, was in her niche,
her breasts as round, her arms as smooth as ever.
One hand went to her heart; the other
lifted a lamp. It shed no light,
for the globe and the bulb were smashed.
The couch in the opposite wall
where Eros used to lie was empty.

He pressed the button of the elevator.
It came, and he ascended—
smelling some cooking soup or stew,
like the smells that waft through a ship.

And when he walked down the corridor
it seemed that he could feel the engines.
These were cabins, dimly lit.
But all the voyage would be inward.
The people who lived here feared for their lives.

Many had moved to Connecticut.
Those who remained, when you rang,
peered at you through a peephole.
Then the eye withdrew and you heard the bolt
      drawn back.

2

It was no grumbling dwarf
or troll who stood in the door,
but Nil Admirari, the Professor.

"Peter," he said, "well well,
I'm glad to see you."

He said, sometimes he thought of Peter
and wondered what he was doing.
Advertising? Well, he smiled,
experience was a hard school...
Peter silently finished the sentence:
"but fools will learn in no other."

What would he have? Mrs. Wilson—
for so the Professor referred to his wife—
was, he dared say, making tea.
Or would Peter like something stronger?

He would? Good, so would he.
And he disappeared to find whisky.

Leaving Peter in excellent company...
all *The Great Books*, with the *Synopticon*,

And the novels of Henry James.
For at that time, after the war,
everybody was either reading Melville
or else they were reading James.
In the words of another famous novelist,
there had been nothing like it
since the craze for table-turning.

3

Professor Wilson was telling his former student
that the visible world was a dream.

The student thought the Professor was the dream.
How could I, he wondered, ever have listened to this?

He said, "If the world is a dream,
then what shall we say dreams are?
We'll have to think up a new set of words.
For there is a difference between dreaming and waking.
Even if we say that life is a dream
that only feels as though it were real,
the feeling is there. We have to deal with it.
I think," he concluded, "we are playing with words."

"That's it," said the Professor,
"that's just the point."
Then he said, in the special voice
like an Englishman's he used for poetry:
"I have seen violence, I have seen violence.
Give thy heart after letters."

Mrs. Wilson came in.
She looked anaemic and had gray hair.

"Margaret," said the Professor,
"you remember Peter.
We are having an interesting discussion."

Mrs. Wilson smiled wanly.
She had seen so many promising students,
and listened to so many interesting discussions.

4

He walked over to Broadway,
and kept on walking, though it was cold,
passing the entrance to the subway.
He wanted physical exertion—the solidity
and resonance of the sidewalk under his feet.

The avenue extended—buildings
with windows, rows of blinds and curtains.

He passed the Far East Restaurant,
a laundromat, a liquor store.

A cigar store...

Then the Calderon. They were playing
Amor y Calor, with Francisca Gonzales.

He looked at the face in the mantilla.
There is always some passionate race
that has just arrived in America.

And a fragrance, *pimienta*,
the wind brings over the sea.

Morning in Padova

Market this morning where dazzling rows
of tiny birds skinned pink, the heads left on,
tell my foreign eyes this scream for raw life
from the death of things may be less abstract
and more Italian than I thought.
Bright tiers of fruit scream too, and meat,
the chestnut hawker and his fire. The world
is screaming, "Don't starve, I'm
a starving farmer" at the world.

This variety of food and in Saint Anthony's,
bones that trumpet from the pillar
loud without a sound, validate man's
weird interior, his hoarded silver,
how he kneels in terror where the lid went down.
We eat good food. We name our body parts.
The skeleton still blows his windless horn.

Padova, I'm proud our Clinton grape
helped save your failing wine. Is your time
coming too? Galileo left and Venice
sinks four inches every hundred years.
You hid all your Jews in 'forty-four.
The ghetto's just a name. We need a name,
not Jew or man but something not so old
formed wild downstream. I hate to bargain
but I bargain for the Giotto yellow
of a pear before bells send the farmers home.
I remain with pigeons, cats, the first bite
of my pear important in my teeth.

Paestum

Life was Greek before Greeks came. The swamp
killed peasant babies, and the local dialect
had no word for hope. Today, old gods
are rooks, more Greek than ever
in and out of pillars that turn ancient pink
late each afternoon. Man always brought
his anguish to the sea. Sealight's best
for tears, and gods can hang offshore
staring you malarial or old.

In 1943 we turned these ruins
into first-aid stations, then gave first aid
to peasants we had shelled. A good wound
makes you cry "Stay with me" at the stars.
How much virgin blood is real
and how much spilled in some old play
on the amphitheater floor? In war
we take advantages to prove we are.

Word's gone back to the commercial world:
if you sail that region, stop there.
You will see our work and you can worship
when the sun is flat and shafts of cream
spray between our pillars from the sea.
Odd dark birds weave through black and pink
we planned. As for natives there,
they farm, die often from some fever
we have never seen, make love
more frequently than we, and when we sweat
erecting pillars, they laugh above their hoes.

IFEANYI MENKITI

Fish Heads

Big head of a fish
wet eyes cooking in the pot

O, I love fish heads
when they simmer

    & English folks
        cannot understand
        why Indians & Africans
        love fish heads,
                eh?—

        in London, the landlady
        got so mad at them
          she threw them
          out of the building
        for cooking fish heads all the time
        and messing up the hallways
          with fish smell

And we have considered the lilies
and how they grow
fed by God's abundant mercy

but the lilies eat manure
and a diet of manure
is not nearly as good
as a diet of fish heads

So let the English eat manure
like the lilies in their Bible;

as for us, fish heads when they simmer…

DONALD JUNKINS

Uncle Harry: Lower Basin 1936

`from the cove, rowing back
alone, the mid-morning sun drying
the pickerel strewn under the seats
of his flat bottomed boat

finishing it off, trolling almost
to the tie-tree, adrift now
reeling in, he spits out the last inch
of his cigarette: get any I ask

thirty-three summers ago, those black
pickerel jaws stiffening in the hard gator
slouch. naryone he grins
throwing them one by one at my feet

clambering up the bank to the fish
table: edging his knife beneath
the stumplimp necks, thumbing down the blade
stripping the skins like masking tape

Uncle Harry: Splitting Oak Before Pickerel Fishing, 1942

        the way he said
it moving his thumb just
enough before the axe

        tossing both
pieces at the pile:
        I heard they was a fire
in the bed this morning
then he left it alone and kept on
with the wood
in one hand, the axe in
the other, cracking it apart, now
and then smelling the grain
        (That morning
I had wet the bed, and skipped
breakfast)

        when they yelled over did I want
anything to eat he had two or three days
fall burning in the pile

out on the water he talked low:
just skip the belly along
like this
        now   one's got it
see there   we'll just sit and wait
till he chews it. You've got
to let them chew it. See his jaws
working. Pretty soon the belly'll be
gone. He'll have the whole thing
in his mouth. Then you can set
the hook. It just takes time.

DAN GERBER

Autumn Sequence

Afternoon
a slanted light
as on a warm October
all you are
pursuing
something vague of apples
ready growth and still
green bracken   a jay
and the first blue haze
juicy with sleep
weight of leaves
a sadness something
long awaited

      * * *

I know the woods
when rain
an hour after the storm
with the wind
a momentary falling
echo
of what has been
a hanging on

Always the same / ticking
on litter of fallen leaves
trying to stretch
the end
something briefly felt
but never
quite the same

      * * *

Splitting logs
is choosing
the proper cleavage
a wedge
can't be set
anywhere
must find
the natural opening / the line
that wants to be a surface

     * * *

Fire must have
an edge to cling to
a place
to spread its forces
a spot
     to work away from

The result
is a matter of timing
place and time / over which
you have no control
the head a sometime pumpkin
full of pith and seeds
that never
     quite
      touch

     * * *

There was a place
together
we spent that last night
apart from all outside
apart from all conclusions
of passing interest

* * *

The duck
wilted in the boat
blood in the bilge
neck strangely twisted
the eye a puncture in flowers

Burn it
burn it all and start again
with less collusion
Each leaf bends into itself
tumbles down and back / spinning
down and back on itself
married to its falling

* * *

Again frost presses
its patterns
silver fossils on the window
I try seeing beyond
the night is nothing
a background
design of creatures
that never die

JEROME ROTHENBERG

Poland/1931: "The Beards"

the idea of geometry is like the idea
of beards an idea of how the light
striking his eyeglasses makes the beards
that hang from their faces
brush the sky   a neglected dream of beards
mad shimeon saw in their glory
sitting in a house of beards holding
the long hairs in his fist
winding & unwinding hanks of beard
oh beards i was your good shepherd once i was
the guardian of all your ringlets
king of beards & eyebrows king of armpits
beards were everywhere we turned
our hands grew beards palms bore the mouths of
    bearded women
mothers whose emblems were a goat & a baboon
who sang about beards & kingdoms old songs of home
impossible avenues forbidden towns where beards grow
hair grew in unmixed colors there was wisdom
in kisses charity spoke first from beards
but was rebuffed by strangers polacks appeared in gangs
ran us through the dawn the sun striking against shimeon's
uplifted eyes who hoarse in praise of beards
made it to the railroad yards but perished
"oh beards i love you beards
"beards which are concealed & beards which show
"beards which begin at earline & go down
"to mouth descending & ascending covering
"the cheeks with fragrance white with ornament
"& balanced to the breastline
"beards of thirteen fountains   sources   dispositions

"first the ears
"second the corners of the mouth
"third between the nostrils
"fourth beneath the mouth from one corner to the other
"fifth also beneath the mouth   a tuft
"sixth ascending from below then rises to the corners fragrant
   at the upper edges
"seventh where it ends two apples grow
"eighth a tress encircling it
"ninth mingled with the eighth but braided
"tenth the tongue uncovered the hair surrounding it is beautiful
"eleventh above the throat
"twelfth the fringes at its base are knotted
"thirteenth hair hanging down both sides a covering for the chest
besides the hair down from his shoulders pure
hippie god of light pure beard & hair
his lineage is in his face a hint of kingship
knowing no god without a beard
he curls the lowest hairs thinks about tomorrow
runs tongue around lips or presses
cool pillow to burning cheeks
a phallic beard is his but on a woman's
    face
         someone calls him
mother of the gentiles others
   are bringing lentils to his room
      still others are kissing his wet hairs
that none will be dishonored none more rich or beautiful
   than these   my strength is in my beard
    he cries my life is in it

how many would die rather than have their beards cut?

ALLEN PLANZ

Shaving with a Dull Razor

Someday I shall lie down
& let it grow
luxuriantly, scratchily
as a xmas tree ready for burning,

host to all that fashion denies,
gold teeth, chiggers, virgins,
a meadow long abandoned
to birds & rusting autobodies.

But now I scrape what resists & hides,
scars of old fights, capillaries
booze has exploded, shapeless fat
frying between a little skin & bone.

What is the will of bacteria?
What is the song of the gene? I ask,
carving my death mask, sighing for sleep

ROBERT VANDERMOLEN

Early

Elbows tucked into the window
(observations from a window)
        Breaking it down
To little pieces on the floor

To smile at nothing simpler

Nothing is simpler
Than order

Enough of winter
The mixed crossed steps
The clouds of slumber

The street made to order
The christian snow
Trackless

Jim I

Sat there
In a folding chair
Awaiting his father:

Sixteen
Is young, if it means
Only more beatings,

Or older
When the boy was ordered
Monthlong to his room last year—

That June crept
By in exploding slow motion; he erupted
July 1st, like a puppy

Ran each four corners
Of the yard, while his mother's
Eyes were gray with tears...

Then last week his father loomed
In the doorway:—so framed,
He was shot four times;

Sound
Catapulted against the background
Hill, the slag-dark ground,

To ricochet
From that squat tannery
Which was the future...

This much older
Boy, is he in second child-
Hood now? Can he recall

More than that he sat there
In a folding chair
Waiting for his father?

GEORGE HITCHCOCK

The Album

Oblong, brown, embossed
with gilt fleur-de-lys,
stiff,
mildewed along the spine.

I open it
and look through the eye
of its broken lens:
clockfaces, ancestors,
towers of dripping sand,
plumed hats,
torrents of shadow.

Music pours
from the holes in its pages—
polkas mazurkas marches,
the songs of the soldiers
my uncles who stood at Ypres
in spitting flame.

In the hot sun of the album
the snapshots fade,
the picnic the regatta
the wedding in the forest
are all blanched
and lost;

glass horsemen enter the album
red-eyed, unshaven,
they twirl their riatas
they lean forward on their pommels,
the weeks and days of our lives
in their lassoes' circle,

while insolent, taunting,
in a crown of cardboard
the queen of diamonds leans
from the album
and calls my name.

DANIEL J. LANGTON

The Girl from Durango

On a burro,
a breast almost free,
she laughed and laughed.
White dress and teeth: brown legs and face: brown burro and eyes.

Sounds in Spanish—such sounds in Spanish.
I tilted my sombrero, making her slow with my squint.
And she was saying: *"Perdiste tus zapatos! Perdiste tus zapatos!"*

She was so beautiful
I decided never to see her again
And lowered my sombrero
Until the bells of the burro had vanished delicately into
heaven.

Noticed

A dog born blind will turn his eyes
Toward you when you speak—
The black moons, distant and dull,
Sensing nothing with the speed of sound;
The head enthralled, between the ears
The brain knowing something is wrong,
Pushing against the eyes from behind,
Sorting the words, judging the tone,
Guessing where the hands are and why,
Waiting at dead center, millions of fathers
With real eyes turning the head to the voice,
Holding the balky legs graceful and still,
Beaming the solid eyes at unfathomed form
While options tingle in unfocused nerves.

EVGENY VINOKUROV

The Light

I saved no facts. I kept no diary.
I hate the particular, details I despise.
An enormous light blinded my eyes
and I saw nothing of what went on.
Years went by. Now, in good company,
I want to speak of what is past, long gone.
But I can remember nothing, nothing at all,
neither the casual trait, nor the subtle shade.
Something, something, no matter how small—
and though I try with all my might
there is only that white and blinding light
slashing my eyes like a razor blade.

translated by Richard Lourie

JUAN RAMÓN JIMÉNEZ

"I Was Sitting"

I was sitting near my table
among my flowers, reading
the bitter and melancholy book
of the poet who knows my dreams.

She came to me silently
and said: "If the poems
please you more than my lips,
I will never give you another kiss.

"Are you coming? The dusk
is so beautiful! Before
it gets dark I want to pick
jasmines in the garden."

"If you want to, we'll go, and while
you're picking jasmines, I'll read
the bitter and melancholy book
of the poet who knows my dreams."

She looked at me sadly; her eyes
with love in them said no
to me. "Don't you want to? I'll go alone..."
Then I went on reading.

She walked slowly, the poor
creature, suffering in silence;
went to the garden for jasmines...
I stayed there with my poems.

She was dressed in white.
Later my eyes saw her
crying and picking flowers
there in the darkness of the garden.

translated by Robert Bly

NATHAN WHITING

Burning a Replaced Farm Home

It was the Kofron's house
to be burned on purpose,
and the Kofrons were there.
The village fire dept. came
with their new equipment.
Children came. The *Hoosier State*
reporter was there. A society
column was being written.
It was a big picnic and
the paper plates were thrown
into the house, and the hog pen
was dismantled and thrown into
the house. Dry weeds were thrown.
It was a good fire—a lot of smoke.
Some thought the firemen
should have put it out once for practice.
The village idiot liked it.
The Gundersons, even though related,
are jealous.
The Gundersons were there.

The Boxer

The boxer tells me
the skull is a good amplifier
for everything that hits it.
His skull is a special blend of iron
and paper.
           We peel the skin off
and see the dark muscles
soaked through again and again
by blood.

FLOYCE ALEXANDER

The Death of Bertrand Russell

Yakima Roy Conant, d. 21 February 1970

Near the end something was caught in his chest
or throat,
so you could hardly hear him tell
for the first time
the story of James J. Jeffries
and how many wives.
It was boxing he loved most
though his friends might insist later his wife
was the subject he never forgot,
the only one he had and left
to hop a freight heading for Omaha
or Liverpool.
Most of those who listened don't remember
having heard him mention Bertrand Russell.

The first time
I met him he was sitting on a stool
in front of his cabin
on the first day of spring.
The bitch dogs were getting chased by the studs,
and the tomcats were stalking the pussys
down the driveway.
He had just repaired Miss Latta's lawnmower.

"I used to get around better
and keep the place up
for Alice.
Last few years my bones don't mesh
so good."

I did a lot of drinking and he did
a lot of talking that day.
He told me about Peter Jackson
and the way he finished George Carpentier
before Bob Fitzsimmons,
and the night Firpo knocked Dempsey
out of the ring. I mentioned Gene Tunney.
"That man was smart. He read a lot.
Some men read and never fight.
Now take that Limey, what's his name,
Russell, he's in the papers
saying our boys are doing the same thing
the Germans did in World War Two.
Now don't get me wrong,

I don't see how he's right,
but by God he's a fighter, that's for sure.
I remember one time I had money,
I bought one of his books.
He said a lot of things in it
I didn't and never will understand.
I don't know whose fault it was,

I guess mine.
I don't read much anymore but westerns...
He said in this book that the truth
is the hunger inside a man
and not just the food he eats."

JOSEPHINE CLARE

Deutschland

"Denk ich an Deutschland in der Nacht
Dann bin ich um den Schlaf gebracht"

"Nights when I think of Germany
Sleep is impossible for me"
　　　　　　—Heinrich Heine
　　　　　　　(trl. Louis Untermeyer)

1

when I

　　swam in her juices
　　drank of her blood

　　ate
　　　　her bones her teeth
　　and hair

　　on whose mind
　　　　　　　　did I feed?

2

she'd gathered courage

crossed the bridge as fast as she could

old man fisheye
hides in the water
with his long iron hook

before she reached home
the second trial:
                    Hydra
flock of geese

3   (the seasons)

it must have been
                    an early cold autumn
mother
when father put an end to
                    your virginity

you said it didn't stop bleeding
still remember the fire
                    in the big tile stove
where you burnt
                    your bloodstained knickers

few weeks later
your father died
his liver in shreds

under snow
you buried your mother
still cry when remembering
(always embarrassed your children)

in march
shamefaced
you hurriedly married my father
                    (bad girl)

with summer
came I
dry and scaly
        fish
                thrown on land

4

long winter nights

they sat round the table
whispering:
       many graves
         many
       had to dig
       for themselves

5

looking up at the sky she shuddered
again
day had turned into night

in which the dead take revenge
the terrible dead beckon gently

the murdered
eyeless
proclaim without voice
the new *götterdämmerung* of the living
                        dead

but in the churchyard
where they were herded together
the prisoners of war
           asked mainly for water

6   (baby brother)

home you came at last
but in a paper nightgown
and a white box

I stroked your head
noticed the cavity in your skull
under the cheap hospital bonnet

and kept it to myself

You had been promised to me
Come O Come Immanuel
I sang in church
brighten
mother's ever clouded eyes
only you
give gentleness to father's voice

Immanuel   Immanuel
I sang for years
prayed you down from heaven

three seasons later now
small body cold outstretched

your weight sevenfold
on my chest

every morning
I went to the train
with mother's milk for you

it didn't do

7

raking hay in the field
she couldn't stop crying

surrounded by flowers
inside
        he lay

the smoke pall
        the sickening smell
hadn't lifted for many years now

strange ashes covered the land

retreat   defeat
        never rehearsed

sun shone disaster

potatoes in flower
white blossoms
opened up   in despair

8

captives
    dressed up as soldiers
looked rather like humans

captives
    in striped cotton pajamas
did not:

they never asked
for our canteens of water
never looked at our bulging aprons
concealing bread

shaved heads bent
eyes cast down on the road
    (a few women, children lined)
they pulled a wagon
empty
    no one asked why

early morning and I woke up
they were passing my window again

now the wagon was filled with hay

and on it lay
their privileged men
on it lay
    their nearly dead

9

*(short song for a village woman
who traveled by train)*

pushed under the seat
the newly born
survived the strafing

only
      his mother
sought shelter
      in vain

10

      she twelve
he fourteen
it was spring

'unconditional surrender'

people in hysterics
schools closed
bridges dynamited

no newspaper no radio
not even a bicycle
little to eat

no matter
they still loved

DIANE WAKOSKI

Love Letter Postmarked Van Beethoven

for a man I love
more than I should,
intemperance being something
a poet cannot afford.

I am too angry to sleep beside you,
you big loud symphony who fell asleep drunk;
I try to count sheep and instead
find myself counting the times I would like to shoot you
in the back,
your large body
with its mustaches that substitute for love
and its knowledge of motorcycle mechanics that substitutes
for loving me;
why aren't you interested in
my beautiful little engine?
It needs a tune-up tonight, dirty with the sludge of
anger, resentment,
and the pistons all sticky, the valves
afraid of the lapping you might do,
the way you would clean me out of your life.

I count the times your shoulders writhe
and you topple over,
after I've shot you with my Thompson Contender,
        (using the .38 caliber barrel
        or else the one they recommend for shooting
            rattlesnakes),
I shoot you each time in that wide dumb back,
insensitive to me,
glad for the mild recoil of the gun
that relieves a little of my repressed anger
each time I discharge a bullet into you;

one for my father who deserted me and whom you
    masquerade as,
every night, when you don't come home
or even telephone to give me an idea of when to expect you;
the anguish of expectation in one's life
and the hours when the mind won't work, waiting
for the sound of footsteps on the stairs,
the key turning in the lock;
another bullet for my first lover,
a boy of 18
        (but that was when I was 18 too)
who betrayed me and would not marry me.
You too, betrayer,
you who will not give me your name as even a token of
    affection
another bullet,
and of course each time
the heavy sound of your body falling over in heavy shoes,
a lumber jacket, and a notebook in which you write down
everything,
but reality;
another bullet for those men
who said they loved me
and followed other women into their silky bedrooms
and kissed them behind curtains,
who offered toasts to other women,
making me feel ugly, undesirable;
anger, fury, the desire to cry or to shake you back
to the way you used to love me,
even wanted to,
knowing that I have no recourse,

that if I air my grievances you'll only punish me more
or tell me to leave,
and yet knowing that silent grievances
will erode my brain,
make pieces of my ability to love
fall off,
like fingers from a leprosied hand,
and I shoot another bullet into your back,
trying to get to sleep,
only wanting you to touch me with some gesture of affection;
this bullet for the bad husband who would drink late in bars
and not take me with him,
talking about sex, flirting with other women,
and who would come home, without a friendly word, and sleep
celibate next to my hungry body;
a bullet for the hypocrites;
a bullet for my brother who could not love me without guilt;
a bullet for the man who would not share his possessions
    with me;
a bullet for the man who wrote a love poem to me
and a year later threw it out, saying it was a bad poem;
a bullet for the man I love who says the only time he knew
    love was when he was 21;
a bullet for the man who says I am a fool to expect anyone
    to love me.
If I were Beethoven, by now I'd have tried every dissonant
    chord;
were I a good marksman, being paid to test this new Thompson
Contender, I'd have several dozen dead rattlers lying along
    this path already;

instead, I am ashamed of my anger
at you,
whom I love,
whom I ask for so much more than you want to give.
A string quartet would be too difficult right now.
Let us have the first movement of the moonlight sonata.
I will try counting the notes
instead of sheep.

Film: Called 5 Blind Men

The poet is not
the blind man/ rather,
he writes
for the man
who cannot see,
                                    making
moving pictures
vivid as walking through a room,
the floor covered with
animate snakes
—some yellow or brown, black,
   a green mamba, corals,
   diamondbacks/
some huge and fat,
others shining, skinny,
short, long—all moving
and looking at him
with flat triangular noses
& fast eyes,
                     Where does he put his foot?

Here is a still from the movie:
black and white film,
showing 5 men standing against a leafless woods.
I am the heroine
of the movie. You never see me,
but I tell you
who these men are,
and in what ways I love them all. I look back
in the film.
on my life with them.

They are all mountain climbers. And that's when
this photo was taken—when they were together
planning an expedition to
Canada.
The photo is one that I, you, the audience,
can find in an old drawer
and remember from 40 years ago, these men now
old or dead, or listed & described in biographies
as their friends,
(like old Hemingway photos).

From left to right, they are
Julian Harmony, stocky, muscular, straight dark hair,
a bristly mustache, always tan from fishing,
wearing a white shirt open down the front of his hairy chest,
sleeves rolled up, the most
articulated face of the five,
with its dark shadows
making you feel he could drink a quart of bourbon
at one sitting and still be telling
good stories;
David Garrison, the handsome one,
the one I have to confess I fall in love with,
standing in front of the tree trunk,
light hitting him as if he should be the hero, of anyone's life,
the only one looking elegant, like a man of the boulevards,
in a light tweed suit, high vest,
sideburns,
his nose flat, obviously having been broken once
but skillfully reset,
a wool tie and you feel there must be,

though not seen in the photo,
a heavy gold watch chain;
Gordon Quails is the center figure,
a brash smile over his turtleneck sweater,
wide forehead; looks Irish,
friendly, has both arms draped around his friends,
(the only man who touches the others)
you can see him in pubs on afternoons,
laughing and telling stories at everybody's expense;
the fourth man
has a fleshy face and a pointed nose like a woodpecker,
round, metal-rimmed glasses,
bangs, a shy smile, doesn't look into
the camera. He is Carl Scandor, he writes poetry
and can name all the plants which grow above
an altitude of 5,000 feet. He looks like
he thinks about god;
at the far right of the photo is the 5th man,
O.K. Ready. His initials stand for
Oscar Karl, but his friends cannot resist calling him O.K.
He's the tallest man of this 5
and is big and bear-like. He wears an undershirt
with long loose sleeves and looks like he's secretly
planning some very devious tricks.
His face has the expression a hawk might have
as it circles over a grain field and sees a
rippling pattern that means a small mammal
is moving through it, ready, if he's fast enough, to be grabbed.

You must use
your imagination

for this film. It is in 5 parts,
each part,
a love poem,
to one of the five blind men.

I. Love Song to Julian Harmony

"And if my sister hadn't died in an auto wreck
& had been taken by the injuns
I would have something to do:
go into the mountains & get her back."

a hunting we shall go,
for the extinct white wolf & the illegal doe,
her belly swollen, containing your sister/
a story the Indians tell
of a lonely white man—he was the moon
his cock stiff, pushing open our eyes,
full of light to shine in the dark woods,
in a smothering of brown leaves,
coupling with a deer,
fucking her, mounting her,
as she moved on delicate hooves, her feet
were the wind that left silver prints,
her eyes were broken branches.

I am stolen
from the grass where I sleep
this warm afternoon,
waking up to a shadow standing over me. I think
for a minute

it is an eagle;
but it's you,
throwing stories over me like fish nets filled with stars
and your mustache hypnotizes the sun,
preventing it from setting/ we are
flooded with day,
your hands are strong enough to push
night away.
You will rescue me;
it is something to do/ to let you
call yourself a man.

II. Love Poem for David Garrison

"The sign said, 'SWIM AT YOUR OWN RISK'
and I did
but everything I've ever done
has been at my own risk"

You told me
you raced cars
until you broke all your ribs,
both your legs,
both arms,
cut up your face
& broke your nose.
                    I
wonder
why
you do not look
broken
or cut

but stand
liltingly
ready to rescue me
from my contract with General Motors.
My feet are swans
that screech at the ground I must walk;
my hands are angry weasels
that crush the necks of chickens;
my face is a bad-tempered carnivore,
a Bengal tiger,
and I only fall in love with men who wear mustaches;
so drive me in your Ferrari
along the boulevards of Paris
and try to win me over
with your clean-shaven face. You
are the one
who's the most adventurous. You only like things
where you must
take a risk;
but inside my mouth, reaching down into my throat,
like a doctor trying to take out my tonsils,
is a sign that says LETHAL.
And we are riding in this car on the boulevards.
Even, without a mustache
you look
so elegant. I have died in an auto wreck.

III. Love Song for Gordon Quails

> "I'll never write a love poem
> so long as there are white plains
> in the place of love"

In this life
I will be a pianist,
I will not have shaky hands,
I will give concerts of Beethoven & Chopin
until I come to a bird sanctuary in the white woods of
    Michigan
and then I'll marry the man I love;
each stroke of my strong fingers,
golf clubs wielded by handsome, mustached, grey-haired
    gentlemen,
will add one note at a time to a piece of music
that will make the world
turn out all its lights.
I will scatter morning glories
around the feet of the man I love. Their trumpets
will be filled with snow from
the woods,
and love will replace words.

You come stamping into the bar,
sit by the fire, drinking your ale. Your cheek is icy,
cool, as I come and sit on your lap,
putting my face next to yours.
My tongue has been cut out.
This is something I've always feared. But
I no longer
suffer from it.
With love,
with steady hands and a keyboard to embrace,
words are unnecessary,

and a love song
is your arm around me,
your cold face.
Chords that take ten fingers to play.

IV. Love Song to Carl Scandor

> "I say to the lead
> why did you let yourself
> be cast into a bullet?"

There is a wooden church on the hill.
It is empty of everything but a woodpecker.
There is a girl here who complains.
She has a bullet in her foot.
She dreams of motorcycles at night.
There is no altar in this church.
She dreams the church service is conducted by ten
angels riding Harley Davidsons.
They are not the seraphim
or cherubim.
They all have mustaches
and they ask her
one question
from the pulpit:
        Will you follow us to heaven?
She comes in with wild flowers
squashed into the mud
on the sole of her shoe.
She answers all the questions,
"Yes."
She loves her god.

She asks him why he's given
her this difficult face.
His angels
even
cannot answer her questions.

V. Love Song for O.K. Ready

> "Each man who dances
> with the bride must
> pin a dollar to her dress"

> "gnawed foot in a trap"

My heart
was caught
in a trap
15 years ago. I have not
like a wise animal
been able to gnaw it off
and run away.
                    To cut out the heart
is to—
this is obvious—
cut out life.

What do you go hunting for?
What guns do you use?
What kind of bullets?
Would you rather die from a gun or auto wreck?
Would you ever resort to traps?

I am a not-very-blond Polack.
I've never been to a Polish wedding.
I've never had dollars pinned to my dress.
I have tried to gnaw out my heart.
Dance with me.
My dress is blood-soaked
and stiff from trying to bite out of the trap.
Where there is love
there is pain.
When I leave your house
I will have to leave
a little blood behind—a footprint on the doorstep.

Forgive me.

* * *

All the men I've loved
are blind.
They do not see how tightly you must hold
a woman
who loves you;   she will
slip out of your hands
like a strong fish.

When I walk into a room,
I see all the men
as potential lovers. I spend my life
writing poems.
Men pass me
like traffic on a six-lane highway.

The men I love
don't even look at me
as they drive by.
They are as blind to my fears
as to my love.
The woman is the camera,
the eye
of the world.

WILLIAM KITTREDGE

Images of Spiritual Parenthood

Flight

HEADING WEST OUT OF BOISE, looking down from a small
aircraft, a twin Cessna at six or seven thousand feet, the crop-
lands near Caldwell are revealed as divided into perfectly
rectangular fields; fenced, leveled, sectioned by irrigation
ditches. In summer, perhaps July, the atmosphere is dusty blue,
cloudless, and the fields are variegated shades of green; alfalfa,
feed corn, brewing barley, sugar beets in rows, potatoes; crops
which are rotated, fertilized, irrigated.

Further west the landscape changes and dries, turns brown-
ish. Across the Snake River and the Malheur, past Ontario and
then Vale, clustered towns, the monotony of recurring lava-shelf
rims and brushy sand hills becomes oppressive. The great shale-
faced two-and-three-thousand-foot geologic fault ridges rise
abruptly and then fall gradually away, sloping toward the west
and the eventual Pacific. On the near side, beneath the steep
eastern fall of those ridges, lie marshy and land-locked valleys
where the white-painted headquarter buildings of cattle ranches
sit on knolls beside the creeks, where water birds nest and lead
their young into spring sloughs already green with algae.

The aircraft reaches the scattered beginnings of timber, jack
pine and lodgepole, just short of the Cascade peaks and the
water-filled crater of Mount Mazama, banks and turns back,
having missed the place it seeks, passes again over Burns and
Lakeview, even smaller hamlets: Paisley, Plush, Adel,
Frenchglen in the Donner and Blitzen Valley; circles the three-
story chimney preserved from the fire which destroyed Peter
French's white frame ranch house—as if circling the memory
of his three thousand head of cattle driven from Willows in the
Sacramento Valley in 1872 when this country was vacant
except for John Devine at Whitehorse, French's death by

homesteader's rifle in 1897—passes the blackish volcanic cone of Iron Mountain and the valley of the Double O Ranch that belonged to Bill Hanley; flies east over Roaring Spring and then over Steens Mountain, Fish Lake and Kiger Gorge, over the Miller and Lux country of the Alvord desert where Chinamen dug borax which was hauled south to Winnemucca in ore wagons drawn by oxen, sights the weathervane on the horse barn at Whitehorse where old man Devine raced his thoroughbreds on a circular track in the 1880's, wanders, seeking the Willowtrail. At last, going east, the aircraft passes over smoke from the mills of New St. Louis. The Willowtrail Valley lies just beyond the timber-covered mountains ahead. The Cessna circles down through heat drafts over the thousand-foot rim-topped ridge on the east side and has arrived. The valley is fenced, ditched, the water controlled, the land contained.

Owning it All

"Give some people the world," the old man said. "And they wouldn't use it as nothing more than a place to read books." Toward the end he got so he'd say things like that, stand there in his only suit, black, as his clothes had been since the death of his wife in 1911, and spit something in his harsh voice and then turn away and that was that.

Maybe it was a result of being alone so much. Anyway, old man Fuller was like those others, Pete French and Devine and the men who'd opened this country, like Bill Brown who once owned 4,000 horses over around Wagontire and wrote checks on the back of tomato can wrappers. Those men got stubborn and set as they grew old and Fuller was like them, surely no exception.

He'd come horseback from somewhere east of the Owyhee River as a very young man, leaving behind no family he ever spoke of, except to say he'd been raised poor, as if he'd sprung from the desert somewhere south of Mountain Home. Actually, in a year-and-a-half of traveling he'd come all the way from the gumbo country around Belle Fourche in South Dakota. Just before 1900 he settled into the Willowtrail Valley, and by the end of the Depression he owned all the flat. What got him the property, he said, was work.

Peat ground cut by sloughs, six or seven miles wide, varying as the eastern sand hills encroached on the meadows, the Willowtrail ran north and south nearly fifteen miles. "No finer property," the old man said, sitting in evening on his veranda porch, talking to his grandson, his namesake, another Carlos Fuller. "High country in the heat of the season and perfect irrigation. Never a dry year."

Moths batted the screens and summer evening began beyond the light fading on the lawn grass. "I went down to Ryolite," the old man said. "Come back with seven hundred dollars from working a season in the silver mines and bought a hundred and sixty-four acres from a man named Sylvan Dixon. I came too late for free land and I was out of money." Then the old man quit talking, as he always did.

It wasn't until the summer he died, 1950, that his grandson learned what happened next. "I went over and stole fifty-three cows from the Indians at Summit Lake," he said. "All of them going to calve. That was 1897. By then the free days was over. There wasn't no Christmas presents." Carlos Fuller watched his grandfather stand and walk stiff-legged toward the door opening into the living room. "That's one thing you'll learn," the old man said, stopping a moment, framed in the light. "That's worth knowing."

He bought them out, one way or another, sometimes getting a half section for only a wagonload of groceries in a hard winter. Mostly the idea began during the First World War. By then his wife was dead and he was raising his only son with a housekeeper, his days centering into work, summer on the desert and winters feeding cattle. It started with the idea there wasn't enough to do. Men were dying in France and he was wasting out his afternoons, working a little on hay equipment and then wandering up to sit by a fire in the living room of the house he'd built in 1906.

It seemed he should have enough work to fill his days, work to tire him and send him to sleep early. And more land would mean more work. In the beginning it was that simple. So he began to think of ways to get more land and after awhile the land became more important than the work.

It came quickly and easily during the hard times of the early Twenties. By 1927 he owned half the valley and owned over a hundred thousand dollars and then in the summer of 1929 he sold enough acreage to pay off his debts with cheap dollars, that one lucky deal sending him into the Depression with no cash but at the same time unencumbered. By the middle Thirties he was able to mortgage the land for government loans and by 1940 he owned all but 900 acres of the valley floor. By the end of the war he owned it all, most of it bought cheap in the midst of failure.

So in 1950, ready to die, he could sit on the veranda porch and look over the valley where the roads were his own, the water, everything, the second largest ranch in Panack County and the sixth or seventh largest in southeastern Oregon. "The best," he'd say. "Best this side of the Rockies." Not the biggest but the best, that was the idea. And in the idea somewhere was the thought that it was best because it was all together, one piece, because he owned it all, all the valley.

The Night of June 17, 1966

He was almost asleep. The long-skirted woman who was his grandmother stood breathing heavily and quickly on the steps, just in front of the screen door, which was even then painted thick white. Clumps of lilac on either side were beginning to bloom and the blooms were dark, purple-black.

He was surprised at her youth. She was surely less than thirty, resembling his daughter, who was fourteen, a fine, beautiful woman who could not have been touched, at the same time seemed frightened or excited and continued staring past him and soundlessly gasping—as if the air could not reach her.

There was one sound. The shot happened. Then he knew where she had been staring, at the long, bluish 30-30 rifle in the arms of his grandfather, Memorial Day, 1934. His grandfather had killed Tom Brotherton with the old rifle now used at the slaughterhouse to kill butcher cows.

It was the noise, the single rapping, that Carlos remembered. An echoless and hostile sound, unlike any shot heard since, singular and identifiable. Carlos was four years old, looking down at the face of Tom Brotherton, who died there, the flesh over those cheeks old and creased and granular, ingrained, as were all the desert faces, with a wind-driven grimace, coarsened by age. A food-stained gray silk neckerchief was tied under the stiff beard which waggled thick with grease and dust. The beard was pale beneath, as if its underside had never before this death been exposed.

While Carlos looked the small entry hole beneath the chin went on pumping blood onto the ground, into the dust, staining the gray silk bandanna and the ragged collar of Tom Brotherton's heavy wool black-and-white check shirt-coat, bright and fresh red. And all the time Carlos was aware of his grandmother behind him on the steps and yet knew she could not be. She died in 1911, before she was thirty, and this killing happened in 1934, years after. She died the 14th of May, 1911.

Nineteen-eleven was a good year, three-foot snow in the lower meadows of the mountains and heavy drifts through the timber and a slow spring thaw. The irrigation water lasted until August. The old man had talked of 1911 and the death of his only wife, of the injustice of that fine spring, the still and tranquil early days of that May, days that seemed endless, as if something had arrived.

Carlos had listened and imagined the early heat of May, false summer before the cold rainstorms of June; late July in the heat and a heavy work-team sweating and moving in their harness and a slow, creaking sweep buckrake pushing hay across a yellowing stubblefield toward a stackyard; drinking water in the dusty, light-streaked shade beneath the sloping planks of the ten-foot-high beaverslide the stacking crew had used even then to lift the hay while they piled it for winter, the metallic taste of water cold in a tin cup.

And his grandfather alone, without the woman he had taken for himself with the idea she would last until his own death, who had borne him one son and then died, and he mourned over that long-ago 1911 summer of getting the work done while reconstructing the reasons for doing it.

...the five-year-old who was his father crying and pulling at her left sleeve, trying to drag or wake her...

She died while hanging the wash on lines back of the house, white sheets and flour-sack pillow cases scrubbed on a rippling metal board, and lay quietly, as if sleeping in the loose spring dust beneath those lines while a slight, warm breeze came down the creek canyon and moved the drying linen. A corner of the sheet she was pinning there trailed a light, curving track in the dust, her wicker basket remained nearly full.

She lay in those old clothes, a yellow-stained apron tied around her and the loose sleeves of a pale green man's shirt pushed above her elbows, the tiny boy who was his father crouching over her. What he saw passed the man in ragged black clothing, his grandfather, returning at last from irrigating, shovel thrown against the fence, the tall pie-faced gelding he was riding, the quickening scenes of man, boy, death for whatever mysterious reasons on a cloudless morning in the center of May.

Watching the child who was his father and the man who was his grandfather while they bent over the figure of the grandmother who died behind the house she had moved into after marrying his grandfather the fall of 1907, seeing that woman dead, watching that, Carlos Fuller began to rise from sleep. In front of the house lay Tom Brotherton, the man killed by his grandfather in a dispute over a red and white bronco-faced, splatter-colored yearling steer. He lay in sun among weeds, mostly Russian thistle, the shadow of cottonwood leaves patterned flickering over the lower part of his body while the sun remained always at two o'clock on Memorial Day afternoon, while somehow his long-dead grandmother stood on porch steps and looked and was frightened.

At last it all collapsed and Carlos was totally awake, opened his eyes, and with memories still fluttering away, saw the almost illusionary square picture frame bedroom window.

Broken Film

In Greece they called it *Ekphrasis*, the still movement. The old man's burial in 1950 was a series of tableaux which formed summations of the past and projections toward the future, contained the past and implied the future, still movements under late August sun. Like an ancient film, occasionally stopped for repairs, the glaring light making it seem as if the incandescent bulb behind everything would soon burn through, as if it all would flare in flaming color on the screen, erupt and be gone.

Shortly after three in the afternoon, followed by almost thirty other automobiles, all with headlights glowing yellow through the dust, the Chrysler hearse from Alexander's Funeral Home eased down the gravel roadways between small, untended graveyard plots, under sixty-year-old homesteader's apple trees and between rows of slowly maturing evergreen, parked alongside lilac near the open hole. Flowers were already in place, horseshoe wreaths tied with velvet ribbons, vases of second-rate drugstore flowers rushed from the small Episcopal Church on the north side of town. The men in the hearse sat quietly, sweating, while the other automobiles circled, waited, parked.

Eight pallbearers, two of them very old, of his generation, the others all somewhere between fifty-five and seventy, the younger men well fed and strong, faces burned reddish by lives spent working out of doors. The preacher, round-faced and balding, maybe thirty-five or six, out of place, an outsider and disregardable, finished his talk. Women were quiet in veils and flowered hats. Then one of the pallbearers coughed, a man named Jacobson. As he gestured at wiping his mouth the moment ended, his white handkerchief seeming a signal, and people began turning away, moving slowly, men in suits, dusty shoes, wives with their babies, children following, old brown and withered hands, veined and liver-spotted, resting lightly on arms enclosed in sleeves that had grown too large, someone stumbles, voices muted.

The glare grew more intense, covering sounds, and in their slow movements, as they talked and pressed hands and smiled secretly they seemed to express contempt for incandescent death. The burial was not their own; a hummingbird paused in the lilac; theirs would never come.

"Dans la lumière du plein jour..."

Dans la lumière du plein jour
Il y a des grottes.

Dans le plein soleil
Il y a des grottes.

Il n'est pas toujours
Mauvais de s'y rendre,

De s'y résumer,
De venir ensuite,

Chargé d'autre chose,
Consacrer le jour.

"In the full light of day…"

In the full light of day
there are caves.

In full sunlight,
caverns.

It's not always
a bad thing to enter them,

to think oneself over in there,
and emerge then

charged with something else,
to hallow the day.

translated by Denise Levertov

Mouettes

Pour elles c'est la faim,
L'espace de la faim

Et le temps de crier
L'espace avec leur faim,

Le temps de promener
L'espace dans leur faim,

D'accompagner la mer,
De maudire la mer

Qui ne sait pas borner
L'espace ni la faim.

Gulls

Life for them is hunger,
vast spaces of hunger,

and time to cry out in space
their hunger,

time to drift
in space with their hunger,

to drift with the sea,
to curse the sea

that will not set bounds
to space and hunger.

translated by Denise Levertov

WILLIAM GOODREAU

The Kennebec's Song

I will cover my body and blood
With layers of clinging sand.

I will wear the nests of gulls
In my hair.   I will make salads
Of shellfish and weed

And bail rancid water from ships.
I will take orders from beds

Of sea hay and garnet-spattered stone.
It will be wrong to want to raise
My voice, make necklaces of tears
Or vow to build a shrine
Of salvaged bone.

Each night I will bathe in the coffin-black sea,
A rainbow's net
                wound tightly in me.

2 A.M.

A dog barks through the horn of a valley.
Low moon burning a cedar.
The creek mutters like an old woman
who walks in her sleep among the trees dreaming
of the life after death
when she will lie down like the stream
and flow to the darkness.

GREG KUZMA

For the Others

Ours is the fate of horses

to be waiting
to bear patience like another skin
to weather dark and slow weathers

and to be standing asleep
along the routes of others.

The field comes up to our feet,
the sky to our nostrils.
The air is cold. Winter is
coming, it is here, it is coming
again.

Inside the barn the straw
is yellow warm, a light
is burning, but the door is
locked.

The mountains
rise behind us.
The ghosts of Indians drape
over the skinny branches
of the ghosts of trees.
They are watching us diminish
like candles.

Below us the tiny houses
rising like a river. The tiny
automobiles scurry in and out
of driveways like prairie dogs.

The freight train we have been
waiting for wails in the distance.

But it will not arrive in time.

Neither will the letters our mothers
have carefully written, the
way women arrange flowers or a slip.
We will not have a chance to reply,
to get things off our chests
with those beautiful gestures of
the drunk.

Nothing is liquor enough.

Blackbirds have eaten the
trees in which we were happy
and waited for winter.

Highways have toppled the fences
we used to leap.

The streams have been eaten by profits.

The wind blows around us.
We are like flags abandoned and forgotten.

Abandoned we shiver like children
deep in their dreams of horses.

Forgotten we honor ourselves
and stand deep in our shadows.

We do no more than anybody would.

TOM GATTEN

Three Poems for the Dakotas

Paul Fish Hawk

He marks the welfare form—
he's painting a necklace for his woman,
Quick Doe, now Mrs. Paul Fish Hawk.

At the end of the line he hesitates,
now draws the marks together.
He's tying a fly for Eagle Fish
in Sky Lake.

Lifting the bag of groceries he knows
that in the old way she's Doe Without Teeth,
since the doctor found gold fillings
in her udders and removed them both.

When the electric mat pops open the doors
he reaches back for an arrow,
and finding none lifts his collar
against the cold.

Across the icy street, he hooks his thumb
to catch a ride back home, where she lies,
writhing in a band of scar,
like a night crawler in snow.

Matthew Yellow Earring

By the leaning barn he loads rigging,
ladders, paint, and remembers
how Yellow Earrings carved and painted
red and black sign-beasts high
along the Mississippi cliffs.
Now he's painted another sign in the sky:

CHEW RED MAN

Halfway home he scales the neon cliff
and works his way down the face
of Doris Day. In a din of horns
he paints Eagle Horse on her white breast,
Bird Woman on the brow of Rock Hudson.
Spotlights skittering all around he spins loose.

Lying in plastic flowers, he covers his ear,
eyes the dripping pictures.

And from the dangling rope sparkles
a yellow earring, some flesh.

John Horse Legs

Boys roar by in a black Mustang bellowing,
"Get a horse, injun," and Snow Beast skids by
on cellophane claws.

He unwraps the new hatchet,
races the engine, and spins from the drift
into Dakota night.

Past the city limit he stops,
chains the doors to trees,
then rears and bolts for the moon,
free of metal wings.

Reaching out he chops stars
from the iced needles of pines.
Ahead, two stars become two moons.

Reining in he's pitched to the sky,
his hatchet hacking Snow Beast.
He floats over moons,
his eyes reeling like poisoned deer.

RICHARD SHELTON

Santa Cruz Valley

again the clouds
which promised rain
break their promises
and cottonwoods
who gambled on water
throw down their paper leaves
in defeat

along a dry river bed
shacks lean against the wind
and dusty light

mothers with dark hair
comfort their pale children
who have no fathers
and take no pride in poverty

one by one the children
will all go away
to dance without veils
to ride a crippled horse
to live with strangers
under the yellow banner of exile

and one perhaps to become famous
years after those he had
wanted to be proud of him
are dead

TERRY STOKES

A Man Called Horse,
&/or Several Other Things

I.

We see the gods mumbling through
their business, tripping

but they are the ones who rip
the spears from our hands,

makes us smile on dusty mornings
when the horses are quiet,

the voices of wolves come
from wolves, this is a good day,

one old woman is always foraging,
another needs a husband, & christ

somebody dies if it gets cold out,
& everything, the ritual, my blood

will soak into the earth, my
blood will be tasted by the gods,

there is no need to speak, speaking
happens often enough.

II.

If you don't find your way clear
on a day like this, it will never

happen. I have seen many men
lolled by the Big Hands, perhaps

even their thighs stroked
& they murmur, & after a while

they are scalping other men, twisting
knives into flesh like their lives

depended on it. Does this sound
familiar? It is a dream we pass

on to the braves as it comes their time
& butterflies sag into the mud.

III.

The day is red. It is red
this day. Red red.

The sun is red. The rocks,
red. Red,

the glimmer, shield of sky.

IV.

I collect my information from the wind,
I collect my information from the heart.

What is murky was murky.
What is a dream but a reminder

of a thousand we've led, beyond
our bodies. Painted differently

& muscles shift, we are soft
& the taste of flower petals

glows through our teeth, a delight
to have been this close to someone

not understanding a word she utters,
not even understanding the subtlety

of a smile, the hips
are a line, the horizon, & small purple clouds

puff like smoke, off there
in the distance, perhaps a thousand years ago.

The rocks suffer, I hear them
mutter throughout the night.

CARL RAKOSI

Poem

The ants came
to investigate
the dead
bullsnake,
nibbled
at the viscera
and hurried off
with full mouths,
waving wild
antennae.

Moths alighted.
Beetles swarmed.
Flies buzzed
in the stomach.

Three crows
tugged and tore
and flew off
to their oak tree
with the skin.

In every house
men, women and children
were chewing beef.

Who was it said
"The wonder of the world
is its comprehensibility"?

"In Thy Sleep / Little Sorrows
Sit and Weep"

In the night
a little crow
whose wing was broken
lay on the ground
and cried out.

Strigidae
the owl
protector of grain
heard
and glided
            soundless
nearby to a low branch.

Straight ahead he looked,
like a man,
            engraved
as on an ancient
            measuring cup
or seated at the knee
of Michelangelo's *Night*,
waiting,
            motionless,
erect.

Not two weeks old,
the crow slept.

An hour passed.
A feather stirred.

Instantly the great
head swivelled
and the bird of prey
                    leaped,

spearing,
and carried off the body
to a distant tree stump.

Again he waited,
                listening.

The implacable beak
then grasped it by the head
and gulped it down.
Three times he swallowed,
spitting out
            the crow bones,
fur, and feathers.

Then the great bird,
silent on Egyptian tombs,
blinked,
            preened,
and hooted.

MICHAEL WATERS

The Eskimos Build a Totem Pole

The head of a moose is wooden,
carved with teeth. Start here.
It will bring luck to hunters
and dogs. Next, frighten the enemy
with an evil spirit. Hollow a hole
through the mouth, let it whistle.
Make the eyes deep. Now an old face,
perhaps a toothless grandmother
left for bears on the tundra.
Eagle's wings and beak, the head
of a fish, the breasts of a woman
shaped with bone. At the top,
your own image coated with the blood
of a seal. Grease the pole with fat.
Reindeer will lick it dry, the sun
make it flame. Praise it.

eskimo grin

from the bone
of this animal
you kill
you make a carving
of the animal
itself.
snow,
like the ghost of birds,
whirls.
you are going to snow
yourself. the dust
of the bone
swirls up
in your face
and the statue
moves, facing you,
without accusation,
small, white,
manageable,
from your skull.
you laugh.
it is yours.
you walk
on ice
as if it were tall
green grass. warmed,
you laugh.

PAUL ZWEIG

Today I Will Admire

Today I will admire the miracle of my body,
That it should know enough to stay alive,
Uninfluenced by the example set for it
In the street, where people are helping
Each other to bullets and strong opinions,
And when you feel something warm,
It is not love, but blood.

DENISE LEVERTOV

Wanting the Moon I

Not the moon. A flower
on the other side of the water.

The water sweeps past in flood,
dragging a whole tree by the hair,

a barn, a bridge. The flower
sings on the far bank.

Not a flower, a bird calling,
hidden among the darkest trees, music

over the water, making a silence
out of the brown folds of the river's cloak.

The moon. No, a young man walking
under the trees. There are lanterns

among the leaves.
Tender, wise, merry,

his face is awake with its own light,
I see it across the water as if close up.

A jester. The music rings from his bells,
gravely, a tune of sorrow,

I dance to it on my riverbank.

Wanting the Moon II

Not the moon. To be a bronze head
inhabited by a god.
            A torso of granite
left out in the weather ten thousand years,
adored by passing clouds.
Their shadows painting it, brushstrokes of dust blue.
Giving themselves to it in infinite rain.
            To be a cloud. Sated with wandering, seize
the gaiety of change from within, of dissolution,
of raining.
            To lie down in the dreams
of a young man whose hair
is the color of mahogany.

ROBERT VAS DIAS

Dump Poem

This is a genuine used poem
last-year's model poem
shirt off someone's back poem
chair minus a leg poem
scrap husk and rind poem
steakbone poem.
You can smell this poem when the wind is right
for miles, around it swoop
herring gulls and great-black-backed gulls,
leaves of a rainsoaked paperback now dry
flutter around it, and graffiti of stripped wallpaper.
This poem is to be thrown out
sprinkled with kerosene
set afire so you can hear its juices
sizzling and its light bulbs popping:
bulldozed, buried, used for fill.

HORACE

"You can't grip years, Postume..."

You can't grip years, Postume,
that ripple away nor hold back
wrinkles and, soon now, age,
nor can you tame death

not if you paid three hundred
bulls every day that goes by
to Pluto, who has no tears,
who has dyked up

giants where we'll go abroad,
we who feed on the soil,
to cross, kings some, some
penniless plowmen.

For nothing we keep out of war
or from screaming spindrift
or wrap ourselves against autumn,
for nothing, seeing

we must stare at that dark, slow
drift and watch the damned
toil, while all they build
tumbles back on them.

We must let earth go and home,
wives too, and your trim trees,
yours for a moment, save one
sprig of black cypress.

Better men will empty
bottles we locked away,
wine puddle our table,
fit wine for a pope.

translated by Basil Bunting

APPENDIX I

Sumac's Covers & Contributors

FALL 1968

VOLUME I, NUMBER 1

CONTRIBUTORS

Neil Claremon
William Corbett
Robert Duncan
Thomas Gatten
Dan Gerber
Mitchell Goodman
Paul Hannigan
Jim Harrison
Trinidad Jiménez-Orrego
Kenneth Koch
Denise Levertov
Rebecca Newth
Raymond Patterson

George Quasha
J.D. Reed
Tim Reynolds
Jerome Rothenberg
Lawrence Shea
Louis Simpson
James Tate
John Thompson
Robert Vas Dias
Nathan N. Whiting
—translations of—
Eugene Guillevic
Nicanor Parra

WINTER 1969

VOLUME I, NUMBER 2

CONTRIBUTORS

Lennart Bruce
Hayden Carruth
Joann Cattonar
Stanley Cooperman
Judson Crews
William Ferguson
Dan Gerber
Donald Hall
George Hitchcock
William Holland
Gary Kissick
Greg Kuzma
Daniel J. Langton
Denise Levertov

Amy Mims
Linda Pastan
Ezra Pound
George Quasha
M.L. Rosenthal
George Shaw
Jon Silkin
Charles Simic
Louis Simpson
Kathleen Spivack
Terry Stokes
Harold Witt
–translations of–
Anghelos Phocas

SPRING 1969

VOLUME 1, NUMBER 3

PRICE $1.50

SPRING · 1969

CONTRIBUTORS

Floyce Alexander
Paul Blackburn
Robert Bly
George Bowering
Alan Brilliant
Clayton Eshleman
Dan Gerber
Alex Gildzen
Jim Harrison
Richard Hugo
Ron Koertge
Richard Lourie
Gerard Malanga
Claire McAllister
James Mechem
Aleksandar Nejgebauer
Rebecca Newth
Michael Palmer

J.D. Reed
Daniel L. Rosochacki
Jon Silkin
Charles Simic
Tom Taylor
Susan Thackery
Robert Vas Dias
Diane Wakoski
Claire White
Anne Winters
Martha MacNeal Zweig
–translations of–
Goethe
Juan Ramón Jiménez
Robert Marteau
Branko Miljkovic
Vasko Popa
Evgeny Vinokurov

FALL 1969
VOLUME II, NUMBER 1

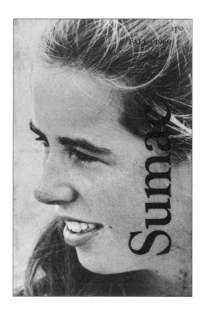

CONTRIBUTORS

Nina Adolph
Michael Benedikt
Sister Michele Birch
Robert Bonazzi
George Bowering
Lennart Bruce
E.G. Burrows
Stanley Cooperman
Jim Crockett
Albert Drake
Barbara Drake
Clayton Eshleman
William Ferguson
Siv Cedering Fox
Dan Gerber
Michael Hamburger
Paul Hannigan
Jim Harrison
Michael Heller
William Henkin

Fanny Howe
Jon Jackson
Dave Kelly
Gary Kissick
Greg Kuzma
Daniel Langton
Denise Levertov
David Leviten
Robert Lorenzi
Gerard Malanga
Arthur Oberg
Toby Olson
Ronald Overton
Allen Planz
Stanley Plumly
George Quasha
Raphael Rudnick
George Shaw
Louis Simpson
Gary Snyder

Terry Stokes
Peter Straub
John Taggart
Ben Tibbs
James Tipton
Robert Vas Dias
Linda Wagner
Eliot Weinberger
James Welch
Nathan Whiting
Andrew Wylie
Paul Zweig
–translations of–
Octavio Paz
Guiseppe Ungaretti
–photographs by–
Siv Cedering Fox
Dan Gerber

WINTER/SPRING 1970

VOLUME II, NUMBERS 2/3

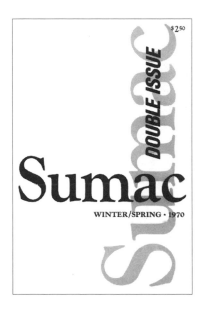

CONTRIBUTORS

Floyce Alexander
Jack Anderson
David Antin
Russell Banks
Eric Barker
Stephen Berg
Wendell Berry
Besmilr Brigham
Rosellen Brown
Roy Bryan
Mel Bucholtz
Josephine Clare
Stanley Cooperman
William Corbett
Jim Crockett
James DenBoer
Clayton Eshleman
Earl Ganz

Dan Gerber
Jim Harrison
Michael Heller
Clyde Henson
George Hitchcock
Anselm Hollo
John Ingwersen
Halvard Johnson
Robert Kelly
Hugh Kenner
Ronald Koertge
Robert Kuntz
Greg Kuzma
Douglas Lawder
Al Lee
Monroe Lerner
Philip Levine
Gerard Malanga

William Matthews
Suzi Mee
Ifeanyi Menkiti
W.S. Merwin
Niall Montgomery
Rebecca Newth
Linda Pastan
George Quasha
Carl Rakosi
J.D. Reed
Adrienne Rich
Daniel L. Rosochacki
Eugene Ruggles
Louis Simpson
Knute Skinner
Joseph Somoza
Susan Squier
Stephen Stepanchev
John Tagliabue
James Tate
Richard Tillinghast
Diane Wakoski
David Rafael Wang
Nathan Whiting
L. Woiwode
Fred Wolven
John Woods
–translations of–
Miodrag Pavlovic
–photographs by–
Dan Gerber
Mike McCormick
George Powell
Bud Schultz

CONTRIBUTORS

Russell Banks
Michael Benedikt
Carol Bergé
Earl Birney
Paul Blackburn
David Bromige
Neil Claremon
Victor Contoski
William Corbett
Michael Cuddihy
Harley Elliott
Clayton Eshleman
Dave Etter
Siv Cedering Fox
Morgan Gibson
James Haining
Jim Harrison
Michael Heller

William Henkin
John Herrmann
Dick Higgins
Andrew Hoyem
James Humphrey
Jon Jackson
Halvard Johnson
Richard E. Jörgensen
Ronald Koertge
Greg Kohl
Thomas Meyer
Kathleen Norris
Michael Palmer
Felix Pollak
Carl Rakosi
J.D. Reed
Michael Smith
Terry Stokes

John H. Stone
Lynn Strongin
Nathaniel Tarn
Carl Thayler
James Tipton
Robert VanderMolen
Robert Vas Dias
Anthony Vaughan
Diane Wald
Pete Winslow
Warren Woessner
−translations of−
Federico García Lorca
Tu Fu
−photographs by−
Dan Gerber
Michael McCormick
George Powell

CONTRIBUTORS

Ray Amorosi
Sherwood Anderson
Douglas Blazek
Edward Brash
Andrew G. Carrigan
Larry Eigner
Clayton Eshleman
Tom Gatten
Dan Gerber
William Goodreau
Robert Hahn
Michael Heller
James Heynen
John Knapp II

Gerald Locklin
Ron Loewinsohn
Jackson MacLow
William Matthews
Robert Morgan
Rebecca Newth
Toby Olson
George Oppen
Stanley Plumly
Al Purdy
David Ray
J.D. Reed
Danny L. Rendleman
Hugh Seidman

Richard Shelton
Alan Soldofsky
Greg Succop
James Tate
Richard Tillinghast
John Unterecker
Jonathan Williams
Keith Wilson
Paul Zweig
–photographs by–
Dan Gerber
John Unterecker

SPRING 1971

VOLUME III, NUMBER 3

CONTRIBUTORS

Mary Oppen
Linda Pastan
Stanley Plumly
George Quasha
Carl Rakosi
Rochelle Ratner
J.D. Reed
John Calvin Rezmerski
Edouard Roditi
W.A. Roecker
Daniel Rosochacki
Donald Schenker
Armand Schwerner
George Shaw
Richard Shelton
Charles Simic
William Stafford
Hollis Summers
Quincy Troupe
T.F. Vandenberg
Robert VanderMolen
Robert Vas Dias
David Walker
David Rafael Wang
Michael Waters
Ramona Weeks
Nathan Whiting
John Woods
–translations of–
Han Shan
Hui Ch'ung
Li Po
Tadeusz Rózewicz
Shao Yeh
Wang Wei
–etchings by–
Mary Oppen
–photographs by–
LaVerne H. Clark
Siv Cedering Fox
Dan Gerber

Floyce Alexander
David Antin
Russell Banks
Stephen Banks
Paul Blackburn
Harold Bond
Joseph Bruchac
E.G. Burrows
Victor Contoski
Michael Corr
Michael Cuddihy
Albert Drake
William D. Elliott
Clayton Eshleman
Siv Cedering Fox
Virginia Gilbert
Gary Gildner
Patricia Goedicke

Donald Hall
Daniel Halpern
George Hitchcock
Barbara Howes
David Ignatow
Robert L. Jones
Galway Kinnell
Linda Krenis
Greg Kuzma
Stephen Levy
Ron Loewinsohn
Jack Marshall
Herbert Woodward
  Martin
Suzi Mee
W.S. Merwin
Paul Nelson
Arthur Oberg

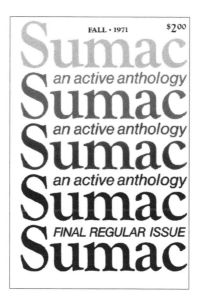

CONTRIBUTORS

Ameen Alwan	William Kittredge	Ira Sadoff
Philip Appleman	Greg Kohl	Louis Simpson
Michael Benedikt	Kenn Kwint	David Jeddie Smith
Jerry Bumpus	Mervin Lane	Carl Thayer
Basil Bunting	Denise Levertov	William Whitman
Marvin Cohen	Tom McKeown	Keith Wilson
Victor Contoski	Thomas Meyer	Harold P. Wright
Wayne Dodd	Lisel Mueller	David P. Young
Franz Douskey	Lorine Niedecker	*–translations of–*
Larry Eigner	Stanley Noyes	Robert Desnos
Kathleen Fraser	Pat Paton	Horace
Dan Gerber	George Quasha	Tamura Ryuichi
Jim Harrison	Leon Raikes	Tanikawa Shuntaro
Michael Heller	Rochelle Ratner	*–photographs by–*
Conrad Hilberry	David Ray	LaVerne H. Clark
Bert G. Hornback	W.A. Roecker	Dan Gerber
R.A. Johnson	Daniel Rosochacki	Robert Wargo
Donald Junkins	Jerome Rothenberg	

APPENDIX II

Index to *Sumac* Magazine

This index records all written materials published in the nine volumes of *Sumac* (I,1–IV,1). Unless otherwise noted, the work listed is poetry. Translations are cross-referenced between the poet and translator. If an author has appeared in more than one issue, their work is listed chronologically by issue. For publication dates of specific issues, please see APPENDIX I.

CLARE, JOSEPHINE

II, 2/3: Deutschland

CLAREMON, NEIL

I, 1: Shark
III, 1: The Note; Starting the Day; Twice I Consider My Country

COHEN, MARVIN

IV, 1: The Saving of Surrealism [prose]

CONTOSKI, VICTOR

III, 1: *Homestead* by Keith Wilson [review]; *Held for Questioning* by John Calvin Rezmerski [review]; *Hard Loving* by Marge Piercy [review]
III, 3: translated two poems of Tadeusz Rózewicz; *Graves Registry and Other Poems* by Keith Wilson [review]; *Relearning the Alphabet* by Denise Levertov [review] [NOTE: A printer's error makes it appear as if the review of *The Immaculate* is also by Victor Contoski—the review is actually by J.D. Reed. See ERRATUM under "J.D. Reed."]
IV, 1: Dead Penguin

COOPERMAN, STANLEY

I, 2: View from the Lions Gate Bridge; Epiphany; The Dybbuk
II, 1: Cappelbaum's Lament; Marlowe's Leap; The Cannibal
II, 2/3: Park Royale; July 16, 1969

CORBETT, WILLIAM

I, 1: "Morning..."; Nostalgia for the Future
II, 2/3: *Speech, for Instance* by Sidney Goldfarb [review]; *Sleep Watch* by Richard Tillinghast [review]; *While Courting the Sergeant's Daughter* by Nathan Whiting [review]
III, 1: Born to This Middleclass Life

CORR, MICHAEL

III, 3: Natural Growth

CREWS, JUDSON

I, 2: No Ultimate Sacrilege; Season of Autumn Light

CROCKETT, JIM
II, 1:   Beach; Ditch Burning
II, 2/3:   Horsefire; Holding Thigh

CUDDIHY, MICHAEL
III, 1:   Noon: Linda Vista Road; Prisoner
III, 3:   Summer Evening in Tucson, Arizona; On a Dead End Street, Looking into a Horse Pasture I Celebrate Evening

DENBOER, JAMES
II, 2/3:   Here Are the Words; Moose Call; The Garden; Old Country

DESNOS, ROBERT
IV, 1:   translated by Michael Benedikt: Nightfall

DODD, WAYNE
IV, 1:   Spanish Instructor Found Dead at Home

DOUSKEY, FRANZ
IV, 1:   Natural Progressions—Unnatural Acts

DRAKE, ALBERT
II, 1:   The 'Thirties as Allegory; Stasis
III, 3:   Addicted to Late-Late Shows the Poet Reconstructs the Past in His Head

DRAKE, BARBARA
II, 1:   She Dreams Herself Titanic; The Ancestors

DUNCAN, ROBERT
I, 1:   Nights and Days [H.D. book excerpt]

EIGNER, LARRY
III, 2:   "to broadcast silence..."; "birds take..."; "moving..."; "It was a long island..."; "the radiator..."; "they keep changing the..."; "the only difficulties, financial..."; "almost falling into the picture turned..."; "the sound..."; "a temporary language..."; "tides off the moon..."
IV, 1:   "To mow..."; "that's the skeleton..."; "an original..."

GERBER, DAN

I, 1:   July, my sweet; A Sequence of Light; Autumn Sequence

I, 2:   *The Talking Girl* by John Thompson [review]

I, 3:   Four from Unicorn: *The Dolphin with the Revolver in Its Teeth* by George Hitchcock, *Snow Vole* by Teo Savory, *Slocum* by Tim Reynolds, *The Torches* by James Tate [reviews]; "Editorial Note," co-authored with Jim Harrison

II, 1:   Gary Snyder —The Intermediary: *Earth House Hold, The Back Country* [review]

II, 2/3:   The Revenant; Isadora; Rounded with a Sleep; The Freeze

III, 1:   "A Note," co-authored with Jim Harrison

III, 2:   On Great Shunner Fell

IV, 1:   Departure

GIBSON, MORGAN

III, 1:   translated five poems of Tu Fu

GILBERT, VIRGINIA

III, 3:   The Pax Romana; Poem About the Minister

GILDNER, GARY

III, 3:   The Farm

GILDZEN, ALEX

I, 3:   For Hart Crane; Roberta

GOEDICKE, PATRICIA

III, 3:   Child's Play

GOETHE

I, 3:   translated by Robert Bly: To the United States

GOODMAN, MITCHELL

I, 1:   The Night Man

GOODREAU, WILLIAM

III, 2:   Laura and William; The Kennebec's Song

GUILLEVIC, EUGENE

I, 1: translated by Denise Levertov: Art of Poetry / Art Poétique; To See / Voir; In the full light of day... / Dans la lumière du plein jour...; Portrait / Portrait; Repose / Le Repos; Gulls / Mouettes; From *The Rocks*: 2; 3; 5; 8 / From *Les Rocs*: 2; 3; 5; 8

HAHN, ROBERT

III, 2: How to Get Out of a Cabin in West Virginia; Getting to Know You

HAINING, JAMES

III, 1: Everyone's River Poem

HALL, DONALD

I, 2: Happy Times

III, 3: New Room; Your Nose; Wood Smoke; "Well, I said, of course..."; "Your tiny..."; "The painting you did for me at Christmas:..."; "I dreamed last night..."; "Loving you..."; The Wine Tree; "Here is the underside..."; Climbing Out

HALPERN, DANIEL

III, 3: Suntans; War

HAMBURGER, MICHAEL

II, 1: Mad Lover, Dead Lady

HAN SHAN

III, 3: translated by Stephen Banks: #56; #10

HANNIGAN, PAUL

I, 1: An Uncollected Note from Professor M --; Notes on Imagery; Laughing

II, 1: No, I'm Not Sorry She Always Says; A Word About Diane Wakoski: *Inside the Blood Factory, Greed Parts I and II, The Diamond Merchant* [review]

HARRISON, JIM

I, 1: A Year's Changes

I, 3: Some Recent Books: *The Naomi Poems: Corpse and Beans* by Saint Geraud, *Gunslinger* by Ed Dorn, *Poets on Street Corners* by Olga Carlisle [reviews]; "Editorial Note," co-authored with Dan Gerber

KENNER, HUGH

II, 2/3: Horizontal Chords [criticism]

KINNELL, GALWAY

III, 3: The Dead Shall Be Raised Incorruptible

KISSICK, GARY

I, 2: Poker — Friday Night; The Fast; August 11, 1968, becomes memorable

II, 1: the beauty poems: Willows; Clothes (and inner garments); Love's Sky

KITTREDGE, WILLIAM

IV, 1: Images of Spiritual Parenthood: Flight; Owning it All; The Night of June 17, 1966; Broken Film [prose]

KNAPP II, JOHN

III, 2: Lillian; Divorce

KOCH, KENNETH

I, 1: When They Packed Up, We Went

KOERTGE, RONALD

I, 3: The Little Girl; The Pig

II, 2/3: Moving Day

III, 1: The Man Next to Me

KOHL, GREG

III, 1: Holiday; Two Lines from the Third Person Diary of Count Vendetta; Count Vendetta & The Universe; From the Mystery of Count Vendetta; Apollo 11

IV, 1: Deathmask

KRENIS, LINDA

III, 3: The Wife

KUNTZ, ROBERT

II, 2/3: The Butcher; The Blood Bank; Dream

OBERG, ARTHUR
II, 1:   Or Image of That Horror; The Childhood Ground; The Balance; Along These Coasts; The Keeper Regrets
III, 3:   The Slowness of the Carriage; WET is for rain; Stepping into This Century; Looking for Doe; Waiting Word; After Loss

OLSON, TOBY
II, 1:   Four Love Poems: 1. after Plutarch 2. after Campion 3. after Herrick 4. after Donne; Barracuda
III, 2:   Relax; *In Time: Poems 1962-1968* by Joel Oppenheimer [review]

OPPEN, GEORGE
III, 2:   Book of Hours; Inlet; *from* Some San Francisco Poems

OPPEN, MARY
III, 3:   "Myself, fugitive..."; A Place

OVERTON, RONALD
II, 1:   Lights; Sharks

PALMER, MICHAEL
I, 3:   "Opening doors, worth forgetting,..."; A Vitruvian Figure by Juan Gris; "Water has worn the island..."; "A small poem about hawthorn..."; For L.Z.
III, 1:   Prose 13 A War

PARRA, NICANOR
I, 1:   co-translated by Trinidad Jiménez-Orrego and George Quasha: Letters from the Poet Who Sleeps in a Chair / Cartas del poeta que duerme en una silla

PASTAN, LINDA
I, 2:   Early Walk
II, 2/3:   Shadows
III, 3:   Dirge; In Doctors' Offices

PATON, PAT
IV, 1:   "At night the..."; "Years waste themselves on me..."; "This ravaged earth..."

QUASHA, GEORGE

I, 1:   Emily Dickinson and the Fox She Knew from Her House;
Nature Scene, As It Imitates Klee; Words for a Dead
Friend; co-translated one poem by Nicanor Parra
I, 2:   Seavoyage
II, 1:   Rilke's Orpheus II / 15; Then; Coitus; Interruptus;
Disclosure
II, 2/3: The State / 1969
III, 3: Total Immersion in the Tank at Allapattah Baptist Church
IV, 1: Thirteen Ways in the Seeing of a Crow; Horseshoe Crabs;
Metapoetry: The Poetry of Changes [essay]

RAIKES, LEON

IV, 1: To Autumn in the Woods; How December is Despised

RAKOSI, CARL

II, 2/3: Poem; "In Thy Sleep / Little Sorrows Sit and Weep"; No
One Talks About This; Leah
III, 1: Americana, 1924
III, 3: The Medium; *Other Things and the Aardvark* by Eugene
McCarthy [review]

RATNER, ROCHELLE

III, 3: Brooklyn Heights—a Game, a River
IV, 1: Solitude

RAY, DAVID

III, 2: Li Po; Dressing on the Sands Where Socrates Drew Circles
IV, 1: Lines for Neva; Russell Square

REED, J.D.

I, 1:   The Chuck Berry Triptych
I, 3:   Strange Kind; Poem; The Quarter-Mile at Flat Rock;
"There are rusted hulks in fiction..." [review of Richard
Brautigan's fiction]
II, 2/3: Fair Game; How Much Do You Charge to Watch Your Train
Roll By?
III, 1: Out from Lobster Cove
III, 2: Last Late Movie; *perimeters* by Charles Levendosky [review];
Good Luck in Cracked Italian by Richard F. Hugo [review];
Laughing by Paul Hannigan [review]; *The Oblivion Ha-Ha* by
James Tate [review]

III, 3: An Empty Bottle, A Broken Heart / and You're Still on My Mind; *The Immaculate* by Allen Katzman [review] [inserted ERRATUM states: "Due to printer's error, J.D. Reed's name was omitted from the top of page 177. Mr. Reed is the author of the review *The Immaculate*."]

RENDLEMAN, DANNY L.
III, 2: A Return; The Veteran; Poem for the Last Poets; Alice in August with Child

REYNOLDS, TIM
I, 1: 7 Epodon: Johnson City

REZMERSKI, JOHN CALVIN
III, 3: The Radio Says Something About Hog Cholera and the Battle at Dak To (I Don't Know Any Pigs but I Remember What We All Remember, That Animals Were Gods Before Men); Poem for the Mothers of New York

RICH, ADRIENNE
II, 2/3: The Blue Ghazals: 9/21/68; 9/23/68: i; 9/23/68: ii; 9/28/68: i; 9/28/68: ii; 9/28/68: iii; 9/29/68; 12/13/68; 12/20/68: i; 12/20/68: ii; 5/4/69

RODITI, EDOUARD
III, 3: Letters from a Lost Latin Empire [prose]

ROECKER, W.A.
III, 3: For a Friend Who Doesn't Read Poetry; Afterward; A Few Hours After Dark
IV, 1: Wife Poem; Being Chief

ROSENTHAL, M.L.
I, 2: Sussex: The Downs; Angels; Further to a Point First Advanced by Walter Savage Landor; Good to the Last Cackle; "Funerals Depress Me, For Some Reason"; This Imperial Day the Dawnsun Calls

ROSOCHACKI, DANIEL L.
I, 3: North Past Newaygo
II, 2/3: Archaeologic I; Restorer III
III, 3: "My grandmother with no English..."; Geneal

Contributors to
The Sumac Reader

FLOYCE ALEXANDER holds a Ph.D. in American Studies from the University of New Mexico. He is the author of two collections of poetry, *Bottom Falling Out of the Dream* (1976) and *Red Deer* (1982).

AMEEN ALWAN's translations of Jaime Sabines are printed in *Models of the Universe* (1995), an anthology of prose poems from Oberlin College Press.

PAUL BLACKBURN (1926–1971) was one of America's foremost translators of troubadour verse. *The Collected Poems of Paul Blackburn* was published by Persea Books in 1985.

ROBERT BLY was the founding editor of *The Fifties* magazine. His recent work includes *Meditations on the Insatiable Soul* (1994).

LENNART BRUCE is the author of twenty books of poetry, prose, and translation. In 1988 he was honored by the Academy of Letters in his native Sweden with an award recognizing his literary career.

JERRY BUMPUS is the author of *The Civilized Tribes: New and Selected Stories*, published by University of Akron Press in 1995.

BASIL BUNTING (1900–1985) was one of the finest English translators of Horace. Mr. Bunting's *Complete Poems* was published by Oxford University Press in 1994.

E.G. BURROWS worked for a number of years in public broadcasting in Michigan and Wisconsin. He is the author of four full-length poetry collections and three chapbooks. His first book, *Arctic Tern* (1957), was nominated for the National Book Award.

HAYDEN CARRUTH's *Collected Shorter Poems 1946–1991* received the National Book Critics Circle Award and his new book, *Scrambled Eggs & Whiskey*, received the 1996 National Book Award.

SIV CEDERING writes poetry and fiction in both English and Swedish. She is the author of seventeen books, including *Letters from the Floating World, New and Selected Poems* (1984).

JOSEPHINE CLARE, a native of Germany, lives on Seneca Lake in upstate New York where she teaches in the local jail system. At present she is working on a long poem encompassing the years 1961–1989, during which the Berlin Wall was in existence.

BARBARA DRAKE teaches creative writing and literature at Linfield College. Her most recent poetry collection is *Space Before A* (1995).

TOM GATTEN's poems have appeared in such publications as *Shenandoah, Colorado State Review, Hearse,* and *Poetry Now.* He teaches fiction writing at the University of Hartford.

DAN GERBER's selected poems, *A Last Bridge Home* (1992) and his most recent novel, *A Voice from the River* (1990), both appeared from Clark City Press.

MORGAN GIBSON lives in Japan and is a contributing editor to *Kyoto Journal.* He is the author of *Among Buddhas in Japan* (1988) and *Revolutionary Rexroth: Poet of East-West Wisdom* (1986).

WILLIAM GOODREAU was born in Portland, Maine, in 1931. He is the author of *The Many Islands* (1961) and *In My Father's House* (1964), published by Atheneum. He lives in France.

EUGENE GUILLEVIC was born in 1907 in Brittany. His *Selected Poems,* translated by Denise Levertov, was published by New Directions in 1969.

JIM HARRISON's most recent book of poems is *After Ikkyu* (1996). His fiction includes *Farmer* (1976) *Dalva* (1988) and the novella trilogies *Legends of the Fall* (1979) and *The Woman Lit by Fireflies* (1990).

JIM HEYNEN's story collections include *The One-Room Schoolhouse* (1993), *You Know What is Right* (1985), and *The Man Who Kept Cigars in His Cap* (1979). "Coyote" was his first published story and has never before appeared in any collections or anthologies.

GEORGE HITCHCOCK was the founding editor of *kayak* magazine. Presently he is a sculptor and painter and has enjoyed several one-man shows in La Paz, Mexico, and Eugene, Oregon.

HORACE (65–8 B.C.) was a Roman lyric poet and satirist.

BARBARA HOWES (1914–1996) gathered her life's poetry in the volume *Collected Poems: 1945–1990,* which was published by the University of Arkansas Press in 1995.

RICHARD HUGO (1923–1982) directed the Creative Writing program at the University of Montana from 1964 until his death in 1982. His collected poems, *Making Certain it Goes On,* appeared in 1983.

JUAN RAMÓN JIMÉNEZ (1881–1958) received the Nobel Prize in Literature in 1956.

DONALD JUNKINS has lectured on the work of Ernest Hemingway at conferences in Paris, Bimini, and Cuba. His most recent book of poems is *Playing for Keeps* (1991).

DAVE KELLY is Director of Creative Writing and professor of English at SUNY Geneseo. His fourteenth book, *Talking to Myself,* was published by State Street Press in 1994.

GALWAY KINNELL is the author of *The Book of Nightmares* (1971) and *Selected Poems* (1982), both from Houghton Mifflin. He received the Pulitzer Prize for Poetry in 1983.

WILLIAM KITTREDGE has taught at the University of Montana since 1969. His latest book is *Who Owns the West?* (1996).

GREG KUZMA's *Selected Poems* is forthcoming from Carnegie-Mellon University Press. Orchises Press will publish *What Poetry is All About* in 1997.

DANIEL J. LANGTON lives in San Francisco. His first book, *Querencia* (1975), won the Devins Award for poetry. His most recent book, *Life Forms* (1995), was published by Cheltenham Press.

DENISE LEVERTOV's recent books include *Sands of the Well* (1996) and *Evening Train* (1992), both published by New Directions.

FEDERICO GARCÍA LORCA (1898–1936), the great Spanish poet and playwright, was executed during the Spanish Civil War.

RICHARD LOURIE translated Andrei Sakharov's *Memoirs* (1990) and is the author of three novels, three books of Russian history, and of the true-crime account of a Russian serial killer, *Hunting the Devil* (1993).

IFEANYI MENKITI was born in Nigeria and presently lives in Massachusetts where he teaches philosophy at Wellesley College.

ROBERT MORGAN has taught at Cornell since 1971. He is the author of *Green Rivers: New and Selected Poems* (1971) as well as the novels *The Hinterlands* (1994) and *The Truest Pleasure* (1995).

REBECCA NEWTH is the author of five books of poetry and is a regular book reviewer for the *Arkansas Democrat-Gazette*.

ALLEN PLANZ is a professional fisherman and a licensed captain. He has served as poetry editor for *The Nation* and his *Selected Poems* was published by Casio Editions in 1996.

EZRA POUND (1885–1972) was right when he wrote "literature is news that stays news." His many books are still in print through New Directions.

GEORGE QUASHA, publisher of Station Hill Press, founded the literary magazine *Stony Brook*. He is the author of *In No Time* (1988) and co-editor of *America a Prophecy* (1973).

DAVID RAY's work has appeared in *The New Yorker* and *The Atlantic Monthly*. His *Wool Highways & Other Poems* (1993) received the William Carlos Williams Award from the Poetry Society of America.

CARL RAKOSI's *Collected Poems* (1986) and *Collected Prose* (1983) were published by the National Poetry Foundation. He lives in San Francisco.

J.D. REED is an associate editor of *People* magazine. He lives in New Jersey.

JOHN CALVIN REZMERSKI is Writer-in-Residence at Gustavus Adolphus College. His recent publications include *The Frederick Manfred Reader* (1995) and *Chin Music and Dirty Sermons*, poems, monologs and skits in live-to-tape radio performance (Magic Word, Box 202, Eagle Lake, MN 56024).

ADRIENNE RICH has published over fifteen books of poetry and four of non-fiction. Her most recent works are *What is Found There: Notebooks on Poetry and Politics* (1993) and *Dark Fields of the Republic: Poems 1991–1995*, both from W.W. Norton.

JEROME ROTHENBERG is the author of over sixty books of poetry, including *Poland/1931* (1974) and *A Seneca Journal* (1978), and editor of many anthologies such as *Shaking the Pumpkin* (1972) and *Poems for the Millennium* (1995).

RICHARD SHELTON teaches at the University of Arizona. His *Selected Poems: 1969–1981* appeared from the University of Pittsburgh Press in 1982.

CHARLES SIMIC's first volume of poetry was published in 1967 by Kayak Press. In 1990 Mr. Simic won the Pulitzer Prize for Poetry.

LOUIS SIMPSON has received numerous awards including the Prix de Rome and a Pulitzer Prize. His most recent books, published by Story Line Press, are the memoir *The King My Father's Wreck* (1995) and a book of poems, *There You Are* (1996).

GARY SNYDER is a poet, essayist, and watershed activist living in the northern California Sierra. His book *Turtle Island* (1974) won the Pulitzer Prize for Poetry in 1975, and his selected poems, *No Nature* (1992), was a finalist for the National Book Award.

ALAN SOLDOFSKY lives in San Jose, California.

TERRY STOKES is the author of fourteen books of poems, including *Crimes of Passion* (1973), and *Sportin' News* (1985).

JAMES TATE is the author of *Reckoner* (1986) and *Worshipful Company of Fletchers* (1994) and received the Pulitzer Prize for his *Selected Poems* (1991) in 1992.

JAMES TIPTON taught for many years at Alma College. He is the co-editor (with Robert Wegner) of *The Third Coast* (1982), an anthology of Michigan writing.

QUINCY TROUPE teaches at the University of California, San Diego. He is the author of nine books, including *Weather Reports: New and Selected Poems* (1991) and co-authored, with Miles Davis, *Miles: The Autobiography* (1989).

TU FU (712–770) is considered one of China's greatest poets.

ROBERT VANDERMOLEN's most recent book of poems is *Night Weather* (1991). He lives in Michigan.

ROBERT VAS DIAS served as the New York editor for *Sumac* and edited the anthology *Inside Outer Space* (1970).

EVGENY VINOKUROV is one of the foremost post-war Russian poets. His work is available in the English translations *The War is Over* (1976) and *Selected Poems* (1979).

DIANE WAKOSKI's latest books include *Jason the Sailor* (1993) and *Medea the Sorceress* (1990), both published by Black Sparrow Press.

DIANE WALD teaches creative writing at Northeastern University and at the Art Institute of Boston. Her chapbook of prose poems, *My Hat That Was Dreaming* was published by The Literary Renaissance in 1994.

DAVID RAFAEL WANG (1931–1977), a direct descendant of Wang Wei, was a poet and translator. His book of poems, *The Intercourse* (1975), is still in print from Greenfield Review Press.

MICHAEL WATERS teaches at Salisbury State University. His recent books include *Bountiful* (1992) and *The Burden Lifters* (1989). The poem that appears in *The Sumac Reader* was one of the first he ever published.

JAMES WELCH is a Montana-based writer whose book of poems, *Riding the Earthboy 40* (1971), has been reprinted by Confluence Press. His novels include *Winter in the Blood* (1974) and *Fools Crow* (1986); his most recent work of non-fiction is *Killing Custer* (1994).

NATHAN WHITING is the author of nine volumes of poetry. An ultra-long distance runner for many years, he recently switched to dance and now performs in avant-garde venues in New York City.

KEITH WILSON's poetry titles include *Midwatch* (1972), *Graves Registry* (1992), and *Lion's Gate: Selected Poems 1963–1986*.

PAUL ZWEIG (1935–1984) was a poet, critic, and professor of Comparative Literature at Queens College. Among his critical achievements was *Walt Whitman: The Making of the Poet* (1984).

INDEX

JIM HARRISON's most recent book of poems is *After Ikkyu*. His fiction includes *Farmer*, *Sundog*, *Dalva*, and the novella trilogies *Legends of the Fall* and *The Woman Lit by Fireflies*.

JOSEPH BEDNARIK graduated from Haverford College with a degree in philosophy. He works at Story Line Press.

DAN GERBER's selected poems, *A Last Bridge Home*, and his most recent novel, *A Voice from the River*, both appeared from Clark City Press.